Memory is the most precious of gifts.


Our memories fade or sometimes become
unintentional in their perspective. Memory can be a
wonderful gift to our hearts and life. Remembering,
though painful, is beautiful.


For there is beauty in the barren…

Beauty in the foreign…

And beauty in the sadness…


Who can understand this kind of beauty?

Kristen ~
  May you find beauty
fur your heart here.
    Candia A. Fisher

# ABALONE

A Story of Two Sisters

Love, Loss and Genetic Possibility

Candra

Fisher

Cover photo by Laura Tobin

Cover and back design by Dan Fisher

To Daniel Fisher,

Who always believes.....

To my sister,

Who always loved.....

"Grief is the last act of love we can give to those we loved. Where there is deep grief, there was great love."

Author unknown

Oct. 2021

PREFACE

"The world is indeed full of peril and in it there are many dark places.

But still there is much that is fair. And though in all lands, love is now mingled with grief, it still grows, perhaps, the greater."　　　　J.R.R. Tolkien

I could not imagine, over 7 years ago when I began this story about two sisters that we would experience a global pandemic followed by riots and looting in the cities across the land.

The world is experiencing collective grief, on a scale, which is unparalleled.

When I wrote about grief, it was personal and close to my heart. As I prepare to send this to the publisher, I realize that this story may help more people than I ever realized. I thought, maybe, if one person reads this and processes their grief, that will be enough.

But now, I realize that there is a world ready for this story.

"Grief is a longing to remember to open our hearts to the beauty of the grief. It is hard. It is sad. It is the deepest loss.

But the light comes.

The light comes when we open our hearts to the light. Loss can linger, dark and sad, for ages, for years…… for decades….. but when we open our heart the smallest crack……. the light shines in."

Candra Fisher

# CHAPTER ONE

## I CAN TELL.....

August 2014


"Blessed are those who mourn, for they will be comforted."    Jesus

This seems to be a promise.

I am mourning.

I am blessed.

I will be comforted.

I will not be comforted or blessed if I do not mourn. I want to be comforted and blessed.

So, I will mourn.

In my own way and God will comfort in His way.

I lost my sister this year. To be exact 195 days ago.

I took my phone calendar out actually counting the days, barely brushing each square on the phone screen and then wrote the numbers 29, 30, 31, 30, 31, 31 and 13 – added them up on the column of numbers written on a yellow piece of paper with a pencil.

195.......So, I mourn.

I mourn in strange ways and the mourning changes.

At first, returning home after the memorial service, all

was still. It was an accepted fact.

Every 4-5 days, I would sleep all afternoon 3-4 hours. Sleep was my comfort. But it was God because I allowed myself the comfort of sleep. I would have never done that before. That's how I knew it was Him.

Now it is November 2014.

I pause and look at the old-fashioned paper calendar and I count again.

I touch each daily square and count aloud. There is something very healing in this process.

247……..

So, I mourn.

"Blessed are those who mourn for they will be comforted. "Jesus

Fall has come, her favorite time of the year. Mine too… Each fall leaf that flutters to the ground reminds me…

Her birthday has come and gone. So ridiculously hard to see, to feel the fall season, her birthday and now Thanksgiving cards in the stores. Every chunky squirrel, every candy corn, every yellow, orange, and red leaf, a reminder. Every small gift I would have bought her.

Tears come to the surface.

Often. And it is good.

I let them come.

I think of her. I will never hear her voice again or get a scrawled note in the mailbox. I will never watch her eyes light up when I give her a gift.

So many "Nevers" but also

So many beautiful memories…

So many…

I am blessed to have had my sister. And we loved, we really loved one another. Remember… that is what the nurse said in the ICU, and it is true. What a precious gift.

More precious than any ruby or emerald. More precious than the brilliant sparkle of the diamonds on my hand.

Most precious…these lovely memories…

Jan. 2, 2015

The first year without my sister in my life. No mother, no father and now no sister. And no other siblings. That was it…just the two of us.

There is a deep void but there is also a strange peaceful acceptance.

I will count the calendar squares again. There is a healing in touching each square with my fingertips.

March 2-written on the little square-Ginny goes to

Heaven..1, 2, 3....29, April....54, 59....May.60, 73, 91 June.100, 111, 121....July.126, 143, 152, August.....158, 165, 183......September......192, 200, 213 October....220, 231, 243....November..249, 260, 273...December..... 277, 289, 304.... January....305, 306.

306 days.

Her October birthday celebrated in heaven. No Thanksgiving phone call this year on the year she would have been able to celebrate Christmas with us, living one mile away. The first Christmas without my sister. 2014…

306 days…

Jan. 3, 2015

I think, now finally after 10 months, I will mourn differently. I will mourn hard....it is my way… Hard. I know that now. What was that mourning before? When it first started? Soft mourning versus hard mourning? I don't know…

This is the hard stuff.

I went through some of Ginny's jewelry to give each one of my daughters… a piece of her for Christmas.

An amber necklace for Nichole. She likes anything that has healing properties since her son, Ansel, was born. Amber is said to have healing properties. It was a large piece of amber on a black leather rope. Really beautiful. My sister had amazing style and taste. She did not think so, but she did. And for Laura, the crow broach. Very Edward Allen Poe-ish…

The crows came to mourn with me this morning. I was looking through her small recipe box, smiling at the choice of recipes… 85% sweets. She loved sweets. I love sweets…the rest consist of chicken, and French onion soup recipes.

I decide that on the day of her passing to glory, this year, March 2nd, I will go out and have French Onion soup in honor of her.

So much honor. Soon, we will discover why.

I looked up and six large crows have landed on the huge barren branches of the maple tree, and they sit, resting, mourning with me. With me, for me, with me…for her.

And I sit on the bed, mourning…I wear the mystic topaz piece that she bought when I was with her.

We were in Mendocino, CA… our place to go and be together, have fun, laugh, talk, eat, walk, window shop, look at the ocean and always buy a piece of jewelry.

This was the last piece bought in Mendocino… the last trip together and I wear it often, as well as the opal ring she wore on her pinkie.

Gosh, I really miss her.

I really miss her.

Jan. 7, 2014

I really miss her.


Jan. 27, 2014

Still missing her and thinking of the March 2nd date that is fast approaching. She will be gone a year.

A year.

365 days. A year.

I love her. It is not I loved her. It is I love her. I love her still and I always will.

The nurse, who did not know us, said it well, "I can tell…. you really loved each other."

So true.

    And so blessed

        To have experienced

            that kind of love

        With a sister

# CHAPTER TWO

## SOMETHING REALLY AMAZING

Feb. 11th, 2015

This morning, as I was searching for a pair of socks, I pulled one pair out and brought them endearingly to my lips and kissed them.

Yes, I kissed a pair of socks that my sister gave me.

Now before you think I have gone over the edge, let me explain.

It was one of the last birthday gifts that she bought for me. She got me three pairs of those expensive, luxury socks. You know the ones… that are in the exclusive shoe stores? They all have the theme of the sea. One was jelly fish. This pair has octopi and fish on them. Really, they are beautiful and high-quality socks. Few people know me like my sister did. I doubt that other people in my life would buy me sea socks.

I don't wear them very often and when I do, it is a "think about my sister" day.

I will keep them until they have numerous holes in them. My daughters will find them when they sort through my clothes and wonder why I kept such holey socks.

There is something amazing about my sister. I could have used the past tense, but I think of her in the present tense when I think about this amazing trait.

She was/is really kind. I mean the kindness that is remarkable. My Dad was like that too! I hope I received that same trait, but really one cannot access one's own kindness. If they do, they know they are not kind enough.

My sister knew about my desire to live near the water…. for years, for decades. So, as we were preparing to bring her to the Puget Sound, we looked for an area that would accommodate my husband and I in our retirement years. Retirement is just around the corner. We wanted an area that we would like and that would meet the needs of my sister. That shared area was Gig Harbor, WA.

This is not the place for the story of this house but suffice it to say it has a "killer" view. My friends would come to visit and say, "OMG, this view is amazing! Why didn't you tell us?" Well, friends, I am not about to brag about the view that we have here, the sightings of the harbor seals and orca whales, the stairs down to the beach, the view of the passage, sail boats, tugboats, and luxury yachts on a sunny day. When the sun is out, the water sparkles like a million diamonds.

It is breathtaking.

We moved in the late fall to our fixer upper house with the "killer view" and Ginny was coming the end of February. Every time, we would talk on the phone, she would say, "Oh Candy, I am so excited for you! You finally got your view." There was such love and kindness in her voice. This coming from a woman who had lived her entire life with NF, raised two boys on her own and worked at a difficult job to provide for her boys. She ended up buying my parent's home and that house became a generational home belonging to our family for over 40 years. It was 1000 sq. feet with a 10x10 kitchen lined with dark ugly paneled cabinets in the junior college area of Santa Rosa, CA. She was content. She never wanted more and was so kind when others had their dreams come true.

She was so kind to her sister. The sister that did not have NF. The sister who lived out her dreams of living in bungalow cottages and doll house homes on five acres. The sister who got to travel the world and would send gifts and post cards from Mykonos, Paris, and Australia. The sister that told her the Tiffany box story. The sister with the "killer" view.

I never felt the merited sting of envy. She was too kind for that.

After March 2nd, which is the one-year anniversary of Ginny's departing; that is when I will start the rest of the story. I will be ready then. I think.

That is when you will learn about NF…. what it is and how it shaped and formed my sister not only physically but also mentally, wrapping a long vine of emotions and pain around her heart and life.

This will not just be a journey for you, the reader. It has been and continues to be a journey for me. The sister without NF.

As I pause and look out the window, the fog hangs low on the water, and I reflect that Ginny never did get to see the house with the "killer view." Even so, she was oh-so-happy for me. What an amazing woman and sister she was.

Amazing.....

346 days; in case you were wondering if I stopped counting. No.

But I will stop counting the days after March 2nd.

Then it will become the years.

Feb. 17th, 2015

Thirteen days until March 2nd.

I have decided to go out to The Greenhouse, a fantastic restaurant in town. I will celebrate my sister by having French onion soup on March 2nd. She loved French Onion soup. We used to get it at the Macy's café in Santa Rosa when I lived nearby. Then she made it and I found her recipe in her recipe box.

This recipe was cut out of the paper and taped onto a three-by-five card. The tape around the paper has yellowed to a deep mustard yellow. It is old....

# Classic French Onion Soup

*Stale French bread is indispensable to a good French onion soup. Two tips: Use white or Bermuda onions, if available. And use Parmesan or Swiss gruyere cheese-never a cheese that will become stringy or taffy-like; these would dominate rather than blend with the soup. Bake at 350 for 20 minutes. Makes 8 servings.*

½ cup butter

2 tablespoons olive oil

2 pounds onions, peeled and sliced (about 6 cups)

½ teaspoon salt

½ teaspoon sugar

3 Tablespoons flour

2 quarts beef stock

2 gloves garlic, finely chopped

1 bay leaf

8 slices stale French bread

2 tablespoons olive oil

2 tablespoons butter, melted

¾ cup grated Parmesan cheese

1. Heat the ½ cup butter and 2 tablespoons oil in a large skillet or Dutch oven; stir in onions. Cook, until onions are transparent, about 20 minutes.
2. Uncover, add salt and sugar, increase heat, and continue cooking 20 minutes, until onions are a rich golden brown.
3. Sprinkle flour over onions, then cook and stir a few minutes to cook flour.
4. Add broth, garlic, and bay leaf. Simmer partly covered for 40 minutes.
5. Place stale bread on a jelly-roll pan. Combine the remaining butter and oil and pour over bread. Sprinkle with ¼ cup of the cheese. Place under broiler a few minutes until cheese is melted.
6. Pour the hot soup into 8 individual ovenproof casseroles, or into a 10-cup ovenproof casserole. Float the bread on top and sprinkle with remaining cheese over bread.
7. Bake in a moderate oven (350) 20 minutes or until the cheese has melted and formed a crust.

I would like to give credit for this recipe but there is no name attached to the recipe.

I can't decide after typing out the recipe; should I go out and order soup or should I make her recipe? I remember having it when she made it for me. I guess I will decide on March 1st-the sorrow month- whether to go out for soup or make it. I will know then.

Oh, my heart.

It longs to find joy in whatever I do that day. Joy in sorrow. Joy with sorrow. Joy over sorrow. Joy and sorrow. Most likely, Joy and sorrow. Mingled, kind of slow cooked like those white onions simmered to a translucent yellow in "real" butter. Always "real" butter.

We will see......

13 days......


Feb. 28, 2015

2 days

I'm glad that this is not a leap year. That would mean that I would have an extra day to wait.

Strange emotions overtake me now. I am glad that it will be a year and I am incredibly sad that it will be a year.

This journey of grief is so unpredictable. It is like traveling to a foreign land. I do not know the landscape, but I have seen pictures. I mean I saw the pictures through the loss of my mom and dad, but one expects that, right? My only sister gone and my parents.

It is a barren landscape. It is a foreign language. It is a sadness to the soul.

It is what it is.

And there is beauty in the barren,

     beauty in the foreign

        and beauty in the sadness.

Who can understand this kind of beauty?

# CHAPTER THREE

## DEEPLY......

March 2, 2015

365 days..........Today is the day.

I decided that I would honor my sister in some meaningful ways today.

I would move my writing upstairs to our bedroom where the "killer" view is the best and I would write today. I am 3 stories high where the birds fly.

Today, this moment, a red tail hawk is hovering in front of me. His chiffon red tail, like a fan, moving in the wind. And tears come to my eyes. My sister's paintings of various birds...... an owl, a heron, a peasant holding a chicken. Other paintings started and never finished. She loved birds. I love birds.

I realize I am rambling today because I really did not want this day to come. When it is just days, I can manage the grief, the bittersweet sorrow. But when it becomes a year or years; it is too long. It is too distant to comprehend.

After today, I will begin the core of the "rest of the story." A story of NF and all its twisted grip upon a person's life, not just any person, my sister, the one that is deeply loved.

NF is Neurofibromatosis.

But today, I made a promise that I would honor Ginny.

I woke up early. I have done nothing and everything.

I watched a fairy tale movie called, "Snow White and the Huntsman." My sister loved fairy tales and had an absolute fascination about them.

Speaking of movies, I went to care for my sister the year before she left this world. It was cancer this time. I wanted to take her to a movie. So, we went to go see the new "Wizard of Oz" movie. Arriving at the value theater, I purchased her a Nathan's hot dog which I understood to be the best. After fixing our dogs with mustard and onions, we entered the theater to discover we were the only ones there. As we sat down, she said with a surprising tone of voice, "I am really having fun; I can't remember the last time I had fun."

A crack in my heart.

I thought of all the wasted time….. not being together. We were worried that we were going to hate the Wizard movie. We both liked it and we both had fun.

Watching "Snow White and the Huntsmen" this morning, I thought of my sister sitting with me watching this movie. I think of the red tail hawk swaying in the breeze, and I am so sad……

Soon we will go out to dinner and have French Onion Soup in honor of my sister.

I slept too. Kind of like the blessed sleep after I got home from California. The sleep of release. It feels different. It is like a long soft dark tunnel that feels like a down pillow. I don't know how to describe it. But it is incredible... this sleep.

365 days.

Like yesterday and so long ago......

Grief is a strange but lovely companion.


April 13, 2015

Wow.... I had to go back and check what the date was. The date of the last time I wrote. Over a year since my sister's passing.

Add to that..... 7 more days and my husband had a heart attack and open-heart surgery. Quadruple bypass surgery......

Surprise!

He is alive and doing well. But all I could think about was that I almost lost him and if you are thinking I am being a little melodramatic; I think not. The area of the heart where the arteries were blocked is affectionally called, in the medical profession, the "widow maker."

Really? The "widow maker"?

More grief to process but that is for another book, another time... not this one.

This is about my sister. Much of the time when I was going through this numbing experience of my husband's open-heart surgery, cardio recovery, and journey, I would think of my sister. I would think, OMG, I am so glad that Ginny was not here when Dan had this heart episode. It would have made her so sad, and she would have worried so much. She would have worried for Dan, but she would have worried also for me. I did not have very many people worried for me and I had experienced the absolute worst thing ever.

It's funny, I really miss how my sister worried about me. She was concerned in a deep way about my life. She was the one person in my life that was consistent in that way. And that is gone now. Gone. I did not have my sister to talk to about Dan and his surgery and now the recovery. She was a good listener. I could call her and talk to her about what I was going through. Her anxiety issues heightened toward the end of her life, and I tried to protect her from stress.

She was there.

She listened.

She prayed.

She cared.

Deeply.

And that is gone now.

So now I am taking another deep breath, another deep longing in my heart to finish and complete something that I see as so valuable. Writing about someone that was a beautiful, kind person which the world could not see.

All the world would see when they viewed my sister was a woman with bumps; some small, some large. These nodules covered her, all over. She hated when the wind blew, large tumors on her head would appear. She had a huge knob on her wrist, sprinkling of bumps on her arms and legs. Her back, that only I saw, was covered with hundreds of tumor-like bumps clustered together. Even her feet had bumps. I could not know how many bumps Ginny had. It is hard to know or even imagine.

Maybe 372, or perhaps 729. But as I considered my back and the area of bumps on Ginny, I made an imaginary count of her clusters. I thought, she probably had several thousand bumps on her body. And more on the inside that we could not see.

My sister had Neurofibromatosis.

And I did not.

# CHAPTER FOUR

## GENETIC SOUP POT

### Neurofibromatosis

The Condition

Because of my deep love for my sister, writing about her and her life is not so hard. But writing about the rare genetic condition that she had is hard, terribly hard.

Here is the definition from GARD- Genetic and Rare Disease Information Center:

Neurofibromatosis (NF) is a genetic condition that causes tumors to develop in the nervous system. There are three types of neurofibromatosis that are each associated with unique signs and symptoms:

- Neurofibromatosis type 1 (NF1) causes skin changes (cafe-au-lait spots, freckling in armpit and groin area); bones abnormalities; optic gliomas; and tumors on the nerve tissue or under the skin. Signs and symptoms are usually present at birth.

- Neurofibromatosis type 2 (NF2) causes acoustic neuromas; hearing loss; ringing in the ears; poor balance; brain and/or spinal tumors; and cataracts at a young age. It often starts in the teen years.

- Schwannomatosis causes schwannomas, pain, numbness, and weakness. It is the rarest type.

- All three types of NF are inherited in an autosomal dominant manner. There is no cure for neurofibromatosis. Treatment is aimed at controlling symptoms and may include surgery to remove tumors, radiation therapy and/or medicines.

**https://rarediseases.info.nih.gov/gard**

My sister had NF1 or NF2. I am not sure which one. She inherited this from our mother. My mother always wore long sleeves even in the summer because of her NF tumors. She had few in comparison to my sister. Having a 50% chance of passing this condition onto her children, NF was passed onto my sister but not me. Both of my sister's sons have the condition. I do not. My husband and I consulted genetic counseling when we had our children. My sister attended and was subjected to a panel of doctors. She did this for the love of her sister, me.

We have two daughters, neither of them has NF. They have eight children and none of their children have any signs of NF.

How can this be?

It can be.

Life is a mystery that we do not understand.

For many years, while observing my sister in the public view; I witnessed the stares, the whispers, and the pointing fingers. Not only of little children but also the ignorant, curious seeking adults. I wondered why her and not me. I had just as much chance as her.

I do not pretend to understand genetics.

In fact ......

I will be very, very honest with you.

I do not want to understand genetics. This is the part of the story that is hard, extremely hard for me.... but get over it, I say. Because this is a story about a sister that had NF and how it impacted her world, her family, her life.... leaving an imprint of beauty and pain for so many.

Beauty that she never saw, pain she felt every day.

The rest of us saw the beauty of her life, her spirit, her kindness.

Why should I write a book like this?

I want the world to know... that it really is the inside of a person that counts.

I mean, we tell our children that all the time, right? But do we really believe it? Do we really experience that? Even saying it aloud sounds so trite.

I had a chance for 58 years to experience it. My children did too and so did my grandchildren. I grew to the point where I did not even "see" the bumps on my sister. Neither did my girls or grandchildren.

UNTIL, her shirt was off, and I would need to help her

with some of the tumors that were bleeding or abscessed. Then I would remember all that she had to endure in a world that idolizes physical appearance. Or until, as the grandchildren and my children got older, I needed to explain about her condition so they would be sensitive and not ask too many questions that might hurt her.

Might hurt?

Did hurt!

I recall a time, one of the young grandchildren poked one of her bumps on her hand and I cringed. I did not say anything, and it passed.

I remember walking in the mall or being in the grocery store with her and children pointing and asking their mothers about her. What did they say? What would you say? She ignored it but saw it. I took my que from her. She seldom made a comment about this sadly common occurrence.

Then one year, in the fall, her favorite season and mine. She told me that she just could not open the door to trick or treaters anymore. I told her I understood and that it was fine, a good decision. But for her, it was one of the hardest decisions. She loved Halloween. She loved seeing all the kids in their costumes. She loved passing out kid candy because she loved kid candy. Smarties especially.

I will never know what happened. She never told me.

Did a pre-teen holding a candy laden pillowcase, standing with his buddies, laugh in her face and ask if she had a mask on? Did a small, darling pink princess point to her face and ask her mommy, "what's that?" I will never know. But at that point, no more porch light on Oct. 31st and no more looking for candy on sale to pass out. Another sadness, another pain for her.

Back to Genetics, I really do not want to write about that. Can you tell?

I remember hearing as I grew up and even Ginny telling me when she was older, that her condition was like the elephant man's. I never really understood that. There was a 13-year difference in our age. But then I watched the Elephant man movie in 1980 and it both fascinated me and terrified me. I was 25 years old.

I was too old to have thoughts like that … all kinds of bizarre thoughts but they were not bizarre for a sister that wondered and worried for her sister. Would my sister turn into an elephant lady? Is this what her future holds? I know that she watched the movie. She never said anything to me. I kept these thoughts in the back of my mind and close to the surface of my heart. I worried for her.

As I was researching NF, I came across an excellent case study called Neurofibromatosis Type 1 and the "Elephant Man's" Disease: The Confusion Persists: An Ethnographic Study.

Legendre C-M, Charpentier-Côté C, Drouin R, Bouffard C. Neurofibromatosis Type 1 and the "Elephant Man's" Disease: The Confusion Persists: An Ethnographic Study. Skoulakis E, ed. PLoS ONE. 2011;6(2): e16409. doi:10.1371/journal.pone.0016409.

This medical journal article written about the Elephant man, John Merrick, explains in a concise way, NF is not what the Elephant Man had, rather his condition was Proteus syndrome. It highlights the psychological impact that the Elephant Man disease had on NF patients, (and sister).

There was nearly a psychological fear that was developed and although I did not have NF, I had this fear for my sister. It was also a surreal experience for my sister. A strange mystical way of thinking of her ....at that time. She was terrified that she might become like the "Elephant Man in the movie" And I was scared for her.

And even to this day…

I have just moved across the bay from Point Defiance Zoo, and it has elephants. I had a membership to the zoo and would take Eila, my granddaughter, age 2, to see the sweet baby elephant. She loved this elephant. Many times, as I gazed across the water, looking at the back of the zoo, I thought about elephants swimming cross the bay toward my house. I could envision them coming across, seeking me out, telling me that my sister is fine, happy for me. She is at rest. And I know she is.

This imagery of elephants is still haunting me today. It is a sweet haunting......

I close my eyes and see them swimming.... I really do.

I looked on Amazon and ordered the Elephant Man movie and a book about his condition. Now, I can have more of an understanding of the impact this has on the NF community.

While researching, I came across this list of statistics written by "The Children's Tumor Foundation" with the subtitle of...." ending NF through research."

### Facts & Statistics

- NF has been classified into three distinct types: NF1, NF2 and schwannomatosis. They are caused by different genes, located on different chromosomes.

- NF1 is the most common neurological disorder caused by a single gene; occurring in one in every 3,000 children born.

- NF2 is a rarer type, occurring in 1:25,000 people worldwide.

- While today there is no consensus, studies indicate that schwannomatosis occurs in 1:40,000 people.

- The Neurofibromatosis are genetically determined disorders which affect more than 2 million people worldwide.

- This makes NF more prevalent than cystic fibrosis, Duchenne muscular dystrophy, and Huntington's Disease combined.

- All forms of NF are autosomal dominant genetic disorders which can be inherited from a parent who has NF or may be the result of a new or "spontaneous mutation" (change) in the sperm or egg cell.

- Each child of an affected parent has a 50% chance of inheriting the gene and developing NF. The type of NF inherited by the child is always the same as that of the affected parent, although the severity of the manifestations may differ from person to person within a family.

- NF is worldwide in distribution, affects both sexes equally and has no particular racial, geographic or ethnic distribution. Therefore, NF can appear in any family.

- Although most cases of NF1 are mild to moderate, NF1 can lead to disfigurement; blindness; skeletal abnormalities; dermal, brain, and spinal tumors; loss of limbs; malignancies; and learning disabilities.

- NF1 also has a connection to developmental problems, especially learning disabilities, which are five times more common in the NF1 population than in the general population.

- The distinguishing feature of NF2 is tumors that grow on the eighth cranial nerve in both ears, commonly causing deafness and severe balance problems.

- NF2 brings on increased risk of other types of nervous system tumors as well.

- NF2 can also cause severe vision problems, including cataracts, retinal abnormalities, and orbital tumors.

- Accordingly, NF research may benefit an additional 100 million Americans (i.e. 65 million with cancer and 35 million with learning disabilities).

- NF is not the "Elephant Man's Disease," although it was at one time believed to be. Scientists now believe that John Merrick, the so-called "Elephant Man," had Proteus Syndrome, an entirely different disorder.
  *"The Children's Tumor Foundation" brochure.*

I am now starting to put the puzzle pieces together of my sister's condition.

My mother, who also had NF, was told she had tumors along her spine. This is what created the intense pain that eventually caused her to become an invalid with chronic pain. She wore a black pain box. As she aged, her brain could not retain anything. Experiencing dementia and addiction to pain killers, my sister watched this happen to our mom.

Most likely, my mother had NF2.

My sister had severe cataracts, balance issues and vision problems in her older age. That would be NF2.

Balance problems began to appear in my sister when she was in her 60's. I always thought it was because she sat so much and was not active. I always thought she could improve her balance.

I thought wrong.

I was ignorant, judgmental, and not educated with the knowledge that she had a tumor on her eighth cranial nerve in one or both ears which would create severe balance problems. That would be NF2.

I feel like a terrible sister for not knowing.

Now I understand that she never had any genetic blood work done. She was simply told she had NF. I never understood that there was an NF1 and an NF2. I am not sure that she understood that.

My mother and my sister with their symptoms appeared to have had NF2, a rare condition. One in 3,000 people have NF1, and one in 25,000 have NF2. The diverse types of NF effect over two million people worldwide. There are more people with NF than cystic fibrosis, Duchenne muscular dystrophy, and Huntington's Disease combined.

Combined......

Yet it seems like one hears about cystic fibrosis and muscular dystrophy more than Neurofibromatosis. Even Huntington's Disease seems to be in the media far more than NF. This baffles me. I do not understand it. I could bet researchers or those with NF do not understand it either.

I want to be done with the research part because I do not like it. (My sincere apologies to the NF researchers. I value your work; I really do, and we need your work) The scientific part of it makes it all too real and sad for me so I would rather tell stories of life and living.

Yet without research and the study of genetic conditions, we are ill equipped to support those with these conditions. So, I see I am not done with this part. It is an education. It is an awareness so that those who live with NF can be honored and understood. We cannot be ignorant even if we want to be...... that cannot be....so we will continue to learn together.

I have learned that my mom and sister had NF2. My two nephews have NF2. I do not have it and my children do not have it. I really do not know how to feel about this. Am I relieved? Sometimes.... of course. Do I feel guilty that Ginny had it and I do not? That her two sons have it and my two daughters do not? Yes.... I have felt relieved, guilty, thankful, confused and so many other emotions cloud my heart in this genetic soup pot. But mostly, I have felt heartbroken for my sister and her boys. Yet and this is the big yet. There has been so much beauty in my sister's life. That is for another chapter.

# CHAPTER FIVE

## A CURIOUS HISTORY

I am done with the genetic part of the story. I know I did say that I would write more… but I am done now. I am not a journalist or researcher. I am a creative writer that wants to write about the love between two sisters. So, at best, I ask the reader's forgiveness for knowing I did not do extensive job on the definition of NF.

I can only hope that by the end of the story, you will see the beauty, the love and that will be enough to touch your heart, moving your thoughts into another direction regarding your perspective. And if you are interested in NF, there is a great big internet world out there and you can read more information about it.

My sister and I were raised by parents who both experienced the Great Depression. My mother's family from Welsh ancestry traveled as Dust Bowl refugees from Oklahoma to the Texas Pan Handle settling in the San Joaquin Valley. There were four children. I look at the sepia tone pictures of the family in front of a bare wood shack of a house. And I want to say I understand.

I have no understanding at all. I just think I do. A little bit like the NF understanding. We do not understand unless we are the one experiencing…. living the life……

What it is like to be hungry?

*I have never gone hungry a day in my life.*

How does it feel to be, like my mother, teased and tormented because she had polio and one leg was shorter than the other? Kids would laugh when my mom ran as a kid.

*I was the captain of the team and, if not, I was one of the first kids to be chosen. I was strong, athletic and a tomboy. Everyone wanted me on their team.*

I cannot even imagine wearing rags for sanitary napkins. Rags......

*I had a special pink Kotex kit that my mom ordered for me, and she talked to me about my period before it came. She was prepared for this time of my life.*

My mother never completed school. Only finishing to the sixth grade.

*I was in my forties when I finished my BA, but I had the opportunity to finish majoring in early childhood development and creative writing. I had the resources to finish school. One of my greatest resources was my mom. She listened to every poem and story that I wrote as a kid. She gave me courage. She believed in me.*

Our mom, at 16 and 17, was working as a live-in housekeeper and childcare provider for a large family because her own family could not afford to keep her at home. Her hard-earned money went to help support the rest of her family.

*I was working when I was 16 and 17. Most of my money was spent on buying cute clothes and shoes. I saved some money to go to college. When I was little, school shopping consisted of Sears plaid dresses, three for twelve dollars, a coat, a pair of shoes, underwear and socks, a white blouse, a skirt, and my mom sewed for me. My mother could have never imagined such luxury.*

Married the day after turning eighteen because her life was so hard. Meeting my dad was probably a saving grace for my mom back then. I realize that is not a politically correct comment to make. But it is a realistic comment. That was the reality of my mom's world.

*I went to college in Southern California for two years, married my husband at age 20 and had my first child at age 22. We were the working poor and struggling but we were never hungry and never without work.*

My mom picked cotton under the scorching San Joaquin sun to make ends meet while she was thirty plus weeks pregnant with my sister.

*I worked at a department store in the credit department while I was pregnant with my first child.*

My father was of Swedish heritage. They owned forty acres of raisin grapes in Madera, California. Sun-Maid Raisins, the cherry- red and yellow box that every kid loved, bought their harvest for many years. And while not well off in the depression, they managed to keep the farm and live off the land. They did not go hungry, but the depression years marked my father as well. He was always frugal. He played football in high school and graduated. He fell in love with my mother.

A severe contrast of worlds. One generation later. It is also interesting to note that my sister and I had a contrast of worlds in how we perceived our growing up years. Remember there is a 13-year difference between us. Her experience was vastly negative and not close to our mother. My experience, almost polar-opposite. I was close to my mother, in fact, best friends in high school. But there was a reason for that as we will come to see soon.

Isn't it amazing how two children raised in the same family can have polar- opposite experiences? It's simply weird. But after talking to other people, I know that my sister and I were not the only ones.

One needs to understand that the environment that one is raised in can affect their world. It does not make their world, but it, indeed, influences it.

Both our parents were a product of The Great Depression. Because we did not grow up in an academically or culturally enriched home, we yearned for that in our lives. Basically, self- educating ourselves in the arts, music, and literature world, we had a thirst for this that could not be quenched. Both my sister and I longed for a cultured life. And we pursued it in diverse ways.

My sister graduated from high school and went to the junior college in Santa Rosa, Ca. She trained to be a psychiatric technician and worked at Sonoma County State Hospital. She had 6 weeks of training and jumped into a challenging world of caring for mentally and physically disabled adults. It was demanding work, but she was always so thankful for her job that paid well and provided for her and her two boys. Her husband left her when the boys were quite young.

He reached over one night and said he could not handle all the bumps on her back......

AND he had met someone else.

This was crushing to my sister for all the days of her life. There was only one man she ever loved after that, and it was my husband. He loved her so and cared for her in so many ways and she loved him. She would often remind me of how blessed I was to have my husband, a loving and caring man. It was true. I did not always see it, but I do now.

My sister worked, provided for two boys that at the time did not know they had NF2. She was a voracious reader, beginning with romance novels and then she went to mystery novels. She always wanted to have a beautiful voice. When she was young, someone made a terrible comment about her not being able to sing on key. It was true, she could not carry a tune, but I loved to hear her sing. She tried to read classic books but never really liked them. She hated sad movies and would not watch them with me. She only wanted a happy ending.

Now I understand why.

She was in her forties when she began to take art lessons. She took several classes at the junior college, then took private lessons for a while. She drew mostly with pencils and blended the colors working from photos or pictures in magazines. She was an accomplished artist without ever realizing it. At her memorial service, only a handful of her friends even knew that she was an artist. She was convinced that she was not.

I loved writing, poetry and reading every serious piece of literature I could get my hands on. I used my writing in women's and marriage conferences. I wrote poetry and dreamed of being a writer one day. Dreamed...... My sister always encouraged me, but I was busy raising a family, working part time, and involved in a marriage-family ministry. I did not have time to write. I would start a million books in my head and was serious about a few, beginning but never finishing. She was my cheer leader.

I was published the year after she passed away and she would have been thrilled. It is sad that she was not able to see my writing in print. She would not have liked this topic. Herself. I could not have written it while she was alive.

But now I can.

# CHAPTER SIX

## GRIEF IS NOT NORMAL IN OUR CULTURE

Sept. 1, 2015

Fall is my favorite time of year. It was my sister's favorite time too. I really miss her during the fall time. This is my second fall without her. It feels like it has been 20 years, not 2 years since she has been gone.

Another fall without us, as sisters, in this world.

I cannot seem to stay focused on this book. First my husband's open-heart surgery and now a very dear friend's husband is on hospice care. There is little to say about that, but a heart and spirit filled with whirling emotions, sleepless nights, unending prayers, and more poems written.

I wrote this for my dear friend after I spoke to her, and she told me the news about her husband.

The Curve of the Moon ****** June 10, 2015


The moon

Dipped into a thick crescent

Reflecting on the mirrored sea


I stand at the window

2:45 in the dark night

And look


And pray

Pray for you - dearest friend


Quietly

I slip back into the bed

The image of the dipping moon

Will not fade


More prayer

　　　More thoughts

Then my heart is cradled

By the curve of the moon


And I know, at once

God who created that moon

Cradles my heart in sorrow, in pain

           And in joy

He cradles all our hearts


He cradles your heart dear one

*"It shall be established forever like the moon. And the witness in the sky is faithful." Psalm 89:37*

So, when I told my daughter that I was thinking of writing a blog about grief, she immediately said, "no mom, that would be so sad for you." Without fully understanding...... it is already too sad for me. So, I might as well go there and go deep.

I am convinced, at least for me, and for most people......if we do not go deep, if we do not mourn, grieve, and feel the sadness to the core of our being; we cannot fully feel joy again.

Sometimes joy is like an elusive butterfly of emotion....one of youth or one-time events; like weddings, babies being born or 4th of July parades; the old- fashioned kind where candy is thrown into the streets and kids scurry to get as much as they can. Followed by fireworks that burst in the air and we do not understand their beauty. But we love that beauty bursting in the air!

I did and do not always understand the beauty found in beauty,

 rather the beauty that is found in the ugly,

 in the painful,

 in the sad......

That beauty is the most beautiful of all. And my sister had that beauty. I am not the only one that thought so.

So, I am going there. And I am taking you with me if you would like to come.

I would like to hope, that if you are reading this book, you were drawn by the beauty of grief, or the idea of living one's life in the shadow of a disease of oddity. Or maybe, you really love the idea that we "really loved each other." There could be a hundred reasons to read a book like this, each one private, pulling inward with a centrifugal force of compulsion. We want to learn something about ourselves, the world, and a woman with such a rare skin condition that none of us can imagine living like that.

None of us can imagine......

I always wanted to take a picture of Ginny's back because no one can fully comprehend the appearance, but I could never ask her. I had been thinking of this book for several years before Ginny passed. I could have asked her, but it would have hurt her deeply. I loved her too much for that. Her ex-husband hurt her, the looks hurt her, everyone seemed to hurt her. Even children hurt her by their curious eyes and pointing fingers. I could not put myself in that category. I loved her......

The rain falls on the first day of September and it fits my mood.

My sad mood......

There are those that think one must never be sad and if you feel it, oh for goodness sakes, good rid of it. Toss it into the sea, throw it far, so far, it will never come back. Why are we so afraid of grief, of sorrow, of the sadness? Why do we not let ourselves dwell in this place so that the healing and joy can come again? If we stuff it, it will come back with a vengeance. And when we least expect it.

Grief and sorrow are a normal part of life.

In the mid-Victorian era, mourning was a part of our culture.  I could have easily lived then. I would have worn black clothing for at least 6 months, maybe a year because I loved her so deeply.  Later changing to charcoal grey.  I would have had a piece of jewelry with a locket of her hair. My mirrors would have been covered with black cloth. Black wreaths would be hung on my door. And I would have not gone to any parties or social events. If this had been my husband rather than my sister, I would have had high mourning, mid mourning, and low mourning, lasting for 2½ years. Mourning my sister was a requirement of 6-12 months.

I decided to look up mourning practices of the 19th century. Here is the opening sentence for a place I did not even know existed. In Texas there is a National Museum of Funeral History.  Their quote "Grief was more than just an emotion for Americans during the 1800s - it was a way of life."

Grief is more than an emotion now… but we do not allow ourselves to fully grieve in our lives today.

I am working on it.

I am grieving.

And I expect to see joy though it and on the other side of it. That will be an amazing feeling. Why would I miss out on that? Why would anyone?

Those around me are worried for me. I smile on the inside. There is no need to worry. This is what will bring healing and joy, a pure happiness that does not come from happy, little over-planned circumstances or activities. Why do we keep ourselves so sheltered, so busy, so far away from grief?

Fear……

The fear of the unknown and the fear of sadness.

There will be a deeper joy, a more relevant happiness if we allow ourselves to grieve.

To be sad.

To long for that deeper joy………


Sept. 15, 2015

In a few days, I am leaving my husband for 15 nights. I am terrified to leave him. I almost lost him. Yet, I know I must get back to some semblance of my life before CABG, (cabbage or open-heart surgery).

So, I am going to Northern California for my grandson's seventh birthday party. I get to help with the party and make a snake cake. That will be wonderful. Last night, I ran into Fred Meyer to look for some pj's for my trip.

I heard a cheerful voice say, "Hello, ma'am.

How are you doing?" By the time I looked up, the person was walking into the stock room. I saw the bumps on her head and neck. There was the characteristic thick neck, and I knew it was NF. I wanted to run after her and say hello and just talk; talk about my sister. Talk to her.

I did not, of course.

It might be so hurtful to a person with NF. I cannot do that, but I wanted to. It might make me feel good or give me more to write about, but do you know what? What would it do for that woman? How would it enrich her life, or would it just be a reminder of her condition?

This sparks a thought that I would like to go to an NF support meeting if one exists, which I am sure it does.

This, I will explore when I get back.

It also sparks another deep sad thought of an incident that happened to my sister. At church, a woman of great beauty came up to my sister and ask for her forgiveness. Ginny was mystified but politely listened as the woman confessed all the horrid thoughts she had about my sister; her looks, her bumps, her ugliness. This woman's insecurities, her perfect face, her flowing blonde hair, her flawless skin, poured out all over my sister, like a soft lotion meant to bring comfort and healing. But do you know what it was really like?

Picture acid being thrown into my sister's face, into my sister's soul. Acid, sizzling, creating deep pockets of hurt. My sister had no idea that this woman had these thoughts,

And this is the point...

People....

This is the point...

If you have bottled up bad thoughts toward someone's condition or life, do not give voice to it. Go to God, not them and confess it. Releasing your thoughts to them might make you feel better, but it may bring deep hurt to them. My sister was so scarred by the acid of this woman's confession; her bottled up secret. For years this hurt her.... She spoke of this incident several times......

Confession may be good for the soul but bring it to God and not to one that does not and should not bear the ugliness of your heart.

# CHAPTER SEVEN

## GLASS SHARDS IN MY SOUL

Oct. 11th, 2015

A dear friend's husband died today. We had been expecting this for over 2 months. He was on hospice care for that amount of time. I told my friend that she was loving him into eternity. What a beautiful expression and what a beautiful occupation for those two months. Yet, the most painful and saddest of occupations. Beauty and Pain again.

This grieving time brings the two together. I delivered a mason jar with a burlap bow that a neighbor had brought flowers in for Dan's heart surgery. I went to the grocery florist and purchased gorgeous yellow roses to place in this simple vase. Do you know what yellow roses symbolize? I read somewhere that yellow roses symbolize memories, good and pleasant memories. And friendship…. friendship with memories…… So, of course, I get yellow roses for my friend because we have experienced many wonderful and lovely memories together.

It is fall again. Ginny's second fall gone from this world. My second fall … without her. Without her. It is harder now. Is it because of all the grief? I almost lost my husband 6 months ago. My dear friend did lose her husband 2 days ago. I spent hours on Pinterest yesterday pinning quotes to my grief board. I have a grief board. Of course, I do. And it is good.

Would you consider a grief board, a grief journal? A grief story shared among friends and family? A willingness to look at the grief in your heart and dwell there. For a while … to process this journey… to walk toward the Joyland?

I feel enmeshed into a season of grief; it is sad, not sad, but SAD……. SAD.

But I do sense the hopeful contrast of grief, joy. JOY on the other side. The other side of what? I do not know, but it is there.

Do you think if you just ignore grief that joy can override and just always be there?

I do not think so…. maybe but it is a fake joy….it is not marinated in the sad grief of life.

It is ok to be sad. It is ok to grieve. Give yourself permission to do this.

I believe in you.

We will be healthier for doing so. Soon, I will be on the other side of grief, but the map takes me to a lingering time in the valley of the shadow of death. Remember that shadows are beautiful, and they keep us hidden in the heart of grief, for a while, and that is good. Eventually the sun comes out, the shadows fade to a dull grey and the sun warms our season of grief.

The warmth is unexpected, and one does not know when it will come. Or if it will come. It will come. Right now…. Is the time of grief and quotes of sorrow.

Grief quotes:

"A piece of my heart lives in heaven."- Author unknown

"Grief is the last act of love we can give to those we loved. Where there is deep grief, there was great love." - Nipsey Hussle

"I'll be OK..... just not today." - Author unknown

"Tears are the silent language of grief." -Voltaire

"Grief.....Grief never ends.....But it changes.
It's a passage, not a place to stay. Grief is not a sign of weakness, nor a lack of faith.....
It is the price of love."- Donna VanLiere

"Grief does not change you...It reveals you." -John Green

"You realize how much you truly miss someone when something happens, good or bad, and the only person you want to tell is the one person who isn't there."- Author unknown

There are sixty-one pins on my Pinterest board for grief and I read many more during this grieving time. For me, quotes help me to absorb the pain, to breathe. My sister loved quotes too! She had many quote books like I do. Now I have books and Pinterest pins on grief, and they comfort me. I will not deny their comfort. I will breathe in their comfort like the crisp fall air on a gorgeous autumn day. That is today.

Yesterday……. did not have that feel to it. My grief hit me like a ton of bricks. I could barely walk through the grocery store.

My husband laughed at me the other day when I described that the sound of laughter was like glass shards in my soul. It is hard for him to understand. It is hard for me to understand. I slept for several hours again yesterday and when I woke, I did not know if it was day or night. I looked to see if my husband was next to me. I almost lost him 7 months ago… remember? I remember every day; every moment and it makes me miss my sister even more. If that is possible.

We all grieve differently but do not laugh or snicker about someone's deep grief. That is very painful. Do you know what is interesting about that? It is not my pain about which I am thinking. It is the pain that someone that I love as deeply as I love my husband cannot feel the glass shards in their soul.

"It's the kind of heartache you can feel in your bones" Or the shards of glass can glisten in the soul of sorrow. That kind of grief. I felt it so deeply yesterday.

Today is another day and I have been considering how my sister loved cooking and cookbooks yet seldom cooked. I mentioned that, and how she loved sweet things like cookies, candy, especially kid candy.

I served sweets at her celebration of life memorial party. This seems like a suitable time to share one of my sister's sweet recipes.

Probably because a sweet can help mend the shards of brokenness in our hearts. Sometimes dark chocolate or a favorite cup of tea. Something tangible, during the sadness....... that kind of reminds me of a quote...a quote is like a sweet....it can mend and speak to our broken hearts. How beautiful is something sweet for the soul.

This was her favorite cheesecake. She swore this was the best cheesecake ever. She made it many times. It is delicious, incredibly easy, and reasonably priced to make. My sister was a fussy eater and complained about food. Especially when we went out to eat.

And, lest you think her perfect. She was the pickiest eater especially when going out. She expected food to come perfectly prepared to her expectations and if it did not, she would murmur and grumble about it. It must have been all those cookbooks that she read or collected but rarely cooked out of. It got to the point where her dear friend, Becky, and I, when going out to lunch with her would tease her terribly, trying to encourage her not to grumble though she would. She would grumble to the point of embarrassment to us, but of course, not to the server. We were the ones that had to endure the complaints.

She never complained about anything I ever cooked for

her. She loved my cooking and always raved about it. A sister's love, I guess. But she got to the point where she would not eat cheesecake from a restaurant. She only liked her cheesecake. It was the best she said.

Ginny's Best Loved and Easy Cheesecake

Typed (and spelled) as she wrote it on the three-by-five card

# GINNY'S SPEEDY CHEESECAKE PIE

Make crust: Combine 11/4 cups plain or cinnamon graham crks crumbs and ¼ cup butter melted. Press into buttered 8-inch pie plate, building up sides. ( *I use a store-bought prepared graham cracker crust* )

For filling: Soften one 8oz. package cream cheese: beat until fluffy. Blend in ½ c. sugar, 1 tbls. Lemon juice, ½ tsp. vanilla, dash of salt. Add 2 eggs one at a time, beat after each

Pour filling into crust, Bake in slow oven (325) til set, 25-30 mins.

Topping: 1. C sour cream, 2 Tb. Sugar, ½ tsp. vanilla. Spoon on pie. Bake 10 mins more. Cool. Chill. Top w/ strawberries

Grief is the season of love and memories. Deep love. And sometimes deep memories of laughter regarding the thoughts of a precious sister grumbling about the restaurant food. She told me at the end of her life that she could not cook anymore at all. She was just out of practice. She had to dump things that she tried to cook. Too funny.........

# CHAPTER EIGHT

## BEAUTY IN THE SHELL

Oct. 22, 2015 and Oct. 27, 2015

*Our Dad loved to go "abaloning." He would leave in the early morning for Sea Ranch past Bodega Bay, past the house where" The Birds" by Alfred Hitchcock was filmed. His wetsuit and crowbar in hand. He would rock pick for the abalone bringing his catch home in a tattered burlap bag. There is an art to preparing abalone. There are many ways to prepare it…. Asian, southern, gourmet etc. My dad's method was taught to him by the old Italian farmer that lived near us in Sebastopol. He loved preparing the abalone as much as he loved" rock crawling," his name for what I term "abaloning."*

"Abalone.

Abalone.   The abalone shell is Abalone

( i/ˈæbəloʊniː/ or /ˌæbəˈloʊniː/; via Spanish abulón, from the Rumsen language aulón) is a common name for any of a group of small to very large edible sea snails, marine gastropod molluscs in the family Haliotidae.

The shells of abalones have a low, open spiral structure, and are characterized by several open respiratory pores in a row near the shell's outer edge.

The thick inner layer of the shell is composed of nacre (mother-of-pearl), which in many species is highly iridescent, giving rise to a range of strong, changeable colors, which make the shells attractive to humans as decorative objects, jewelry, and as a source of colorful mother-of-pearl.

The exterior of the shell is striated and dull. The color of the shell is very variable from species to species which may reflect the animal's diet. The iridescent nacre that lines the inside of the shell varies in color from silvery white, to pink, red and green-red to deep blue, green to purple." "Abalone" (Wikipedia)

*The abalone shell is quite ugly on the outside. A dull red color with abrasive bumps on the exterior. I was really horrified the first time I realized how much my sister was like the abalone shell. She too, my sister, had bumps all on the outside of her skin....... she was dull, ugly, and bumpy by the world's standards.*

*But have you ever seen the inside of an abalone shell? It is absolutely the most beautiful iridescent shell with hues of color; peacock blue, sage green, royal purple, and swirly pinky- peach tones that capture the heart....and creates a certain ethereal beauty. Each shell, unique, inside, and out. The colors mingle into the most beautiful patterns creating some of the most gorgeous jewelry. I am going to put a necklace on now. It was Ginny's –we both bought one together at a shop on the way home from Mendocino, CA. I wear the piece she picked out, beautiful in its own way, a rusty red exterior; the other side, in contrast, an iridescent shimmer of the sea... next to my heart. She is so near to my*

*heart today. Her necklace is the most beautiful. Of the two necklaces, it is the roughest and rustic. It represents the real beauty and ugliness of the abalone. It represents her.........*
*I told you that I could have never written this while she was alive on this earth.*

"The shell of the abalone is exceptionally strong and is made of microscopic calcium carbonate tiles stacked like bricks. Between the layers of tiles is a clingy protein substance. When the abalone shell is struck, the tiles slide instead of shattering and the protein stretches to absorb the energy of the blow. Material scientists around the world are studying this tiled structure for insight into stronger ceramic products such as body armor. The dust created by grinding and cutting abalone shell is dangerous; appropriate safeguards must be taken to protect people from inhaling these particles." "Abalone" (Wikipedia)

*How fascinating this is; like my sister, struck down by the standards of beauty that this world held; children pointing at her and asking their mommies about "that lady;" adults, unashamedly, staring at her to the point of disbelief.*

*I was with her, I saw this. She would pretend it did not happen. But I felt the sting of the blows sent her way. She was struck with these gazes and stares all through her 71 years.*

*Maybe beginning in her teen years when the bumps began to show. She had to absorb the negative energy of stares, the*

*adjunct horror.... absorbing that all into her heart and spirit
like a blow. How many times did she shatter?? Appearing
resilient, she would continue... going out into public, eating
lunch, going to church, the dentist and Macy's like everyone
else. But the feeling of the "sideshow" aspect of her life was
there, ever present, on the surface of her life, on the surface of
her skin.*

"The meat (foot muscle) of abalone is used for food,
and the shells of abalone are used as decorative items
and as a source of mother of pearl for jewelry, buttons,
buckles, and inlay.

The flesh of abalones is widely considered to be a
desirable food and is consumed raw or cooked in a
variety of cultures." "Abalone" (Wikipedia)

*The foot or muscle of the abalone is popped out of the shell,
the pink or greenish guts cleaned out, the bottom foot and
black epipodium are cut off with the sharpest knife possible.
The muscle is tough and strong, of creamish color, and it is
essential to tenderize before eating. One slices the foot into
thin slices, then you use a meat mallet to tenderize the meat
on both sides. At this point, the abalone could be stored in
the freezer and some of it was. But there would always be a
nice big batch of abalone to make an amazing meal. Even, as
a kid and teen, I was so used to these meals, that I did not
understand that abalone was a delicacy. At that time, the
meat was selling for thirty-five dollars a pound. Today, you
can find fresh abalone steaks for $90 to $155 dollars a pound.*

"Farming of abalone began in the late 1950s and early 1960s in Japan and China. Since the mid-1990s, there have been many increasingly successful endeavors to commercially farm abalone for the purpose of consumption. Overfishing and poaching have reduced wild populations to such an extent that farmed abalone now supplies most of the abalone meat consumed." "Abalone" (Wikipedia)

*Now, put 2-3 eggs in a pie dish, beat with some milk, dip the tenderized abalone steak in the egg mixture, cover both sides with finely crushed saltines, fry in Wesson oil on a hot temperature until golden brown on both sides. We fried ours outside under the covered patio. My mom did not like the smell getting into the house. And this was my dad's domain to cook "stinky fish." Eaten hot with vegetables from the garden and ice cream often hand cranked but store bought as my dad got older.*

*The taste; tender, golden crispy brown with the taste of mild fish or chicken. It would melt in your mouth.*

*How I would love to have some of that abalone today. I can almost imagine the taste of it. The time spent with family over an abalone dinner, then taken for granted, now such a treasured memory.*

*I have two barrels of abalone shells. Accumulated at my sisters' home from the many days of my fathers' sport for the precious meat. He loved his abalone shells. He hung them with wire on the back-yard fence. I thought it was tasteless looking for the longest time.*

*Now I see it as sweet and enduring. How our emotions and perspective changes with time. My plan is to have an outside coffee table made with the abalone shells underneath a sheet of glass…. a constant reminder of the beauty in the shell and the outer dismay of the ugliness. It is the inner beauty of the shell that captures you, it is the inner beauty of the person that captures you……. I miss that inner beauty every single day that my sister is gone.*

Oct. 30, 2015

The second Halloween without Ginny. I may miss her more this year than last. I am not sure why. The striking realization that she is really gone……. So hard. This week, I have been so sad that my husband and a good friend are questioning my frame of mind. I know they are worried. I am not worried.

I want to scream at them that they do not understand, and they do not. I tell them that this is normal, natural –what all of us should experience when we are in a mourning season. My friend was like this when she lost her daughter. She understands the rawness of it. That this tender wounding lasts an enduringly long time. Our hearts experience the deep depth of grief.

My husband is wondering if he should somehow intervene and help me through this and I am saying no.

I try to tell them that this will pass. I have lost my

sister, my parents, well over a decade before. My dear friend's husband passed, and my husband almost died this year. A litany of loss. I am writing about grief and sorrow.

I must reassure them. That takes effort too.

I am bone weary with grief.

And that's ok. It is as it should be. Let me process this people. Please let me do this grief… in my time.

On my time frame not yours…….

I really believe in our culture that people are non-accepting of grief. They are more tolerant of death than of the grief that follows.

If one person reads this and can settle into their grief season to grieve well, I will be so happy. At peace for the words and feelings that are shared. For the person that hears my heart, they can grieve within resting in their own contented grief season.

Do not let anyone take this grieving season from you. Stomp your feet, set your heart and be at peace with your grief. It will pass but in its own time.

# CHAPTER NINE

## THE COLLECTOR, THE ARTIST AND THE SOUL BEAUTY OF A SISTER......

The leaves are swirling again. The sun touches the peninsula point of Colvos Passage. High dark clouds hang in the sky. It is deeply beautiful today. A day that my sister would like.

My sister drew the heavy brocade curtains closed so sunshine would not come into her home. I would waltz in and open the drapes. I did not always respect or honor her way of being. I thought she needed sunshine. She collected pictures that were darkly foreboding.... dark trees or dark charcoal skies above golden hayfields. There was something in the dark that called to her. I think it might have been the shadow aspect. The idea of hiding in the shadows, within a world, brightly illuminating the misfits of this world. Shining on the elephant people, the children with cleft palates she sent money to, the ugly exteriors of what the world perceives grotesque without going deeper into the person, the story, the spirit, the soul.

She loved dark pictures on her walls. She loved dark antique furniture. She had the taste of a natural wealthy baroness. She only bought what she loved and put it together and I am serious when I say, it looked like it belonged in an Architectural Digest or House Beautiful magazine. This is the inner beauty of style that she had. I wish I had a picture of her living room to show you. It lives in my brain like a sepia print from long ago. Every time, I walked into my sister's home, I felt her and knew her a little bit more. People do not know how to decorate like that anymore. They just do not…the trend is all Pottery Barn or mid-century modern, hotel-looking, the Farmhouse style. It is not who they are, nor does it represent their personality. They are just a copycat out of a magazine or an HGTV show.

My sister was never a copycat. She was herself. There is so much beauty in that. She did not always want to be the exterior her. Sometimes she made comments that were like daggers to my heart. Seldom said so even the more poignant. Said to me, the sister with the pure complexion, the one who had two children without NF, and she had two sons with it.

My heart broke for her at those moments.

My sister loved collecting antiques and vintage items. I encouraged her to consider, when she retired, to start a small booth at an antique mall. This was in the prosperous 80's and 90's when antiques were expensive in Northern California. When she would come to visit, we would go antiquing to Snohomish, Centralia, Bothell, and Olympia, finding many treasures. As we grew older, some of our tastes began to overlap and we would laugh if one found something that the other one would like. We would teasingly fight over who "saw it" first.

I have many of her items. I have her red Asian-style

dresser with all the little drawers, her original artist pictures from a Bodega Bay gallery, her expensive chartreuse-green tv cabinet, her honey-colored bookcases in the beach room, her kaleidoscopes, her fish plates, her Vitamix blender, all her artwork.

I am surrounded by her, and I love that.

We painted her walls, Monet's Haystack Yellow, in the living and dining room and Martha Stewart's Hollyhock Red for her bedroom. She wanted me to pick the colors. We tried to paint the Holly Hock walls but having issues with our neck and arms, we hired a painter. We laughed.


Nov. 5, 2015

October is over. Now the thought of Christmas. This is the 2nd Christmas without her. I loved looking for the perfect gifts for Ginny. I went to Marshalls to try to find something to wear to my friend's memorial service and could not find anything, but I found a million gifts for Ginny. Pajamas, soft ones…. I used to make her long flannel nightgowns and she loved them. She wore them until they were threadbare. I have a nightgown she gave me, a Scottie dog nightgown. She really is the only one that knows how much I love Scottie dogs. Socks, scarves, sweaters, oh my and oh sad.

Will this feeling ever pass?

It may soften with time but never pass...not completely.

Some would make it pass so they could move on without the sadness.

The sadness is making me who I will become for the rest of my days, and I welcome that. I do not want to push the sadness away. Balance is important. I get that.

Last night I was invited to a new neighbor's house, to meet her and enjoy some wine. I was just too sad to go. The memorial service of my dear friend's husband is tomorrow. My shopping excursion put me over the edge into a sad world. I did not want to subject my new neighbor to this. It would not be a representation of me, or would it? I am changing, becoming melancholy, more of an introvert.

I have read that a writer can be an introvert and that it is a lonely profession. I have never written seriously until now. I can see it; feel it.

My past, present and, God willing, the future is creating me. I can accept that. I am not sure others can. Perhaps my world will provide new people and friends that can understand this sadness.


Nov. 9, 2015

I sit in the van with Eila, my adorable 3-year-old granddaughter. Her mommy runs into the store to get something, and I look at the fall trees with the autumn leaves falling and I begin to sing the song that I used to teach the kindergarteners- "Autumn leaves now are falling, red and yellow and brown, Autumn leaves now are falling....watch them touch the ground." We taught the children to sway and twirl as they sang the song. Eila likes the melodic song as I sing it over and over. She hums and sings the ending words. And I smile and am happy to sing this little song with her. I love fall. This was just a few days ago.

But not today. I gaze out of the third story window of my house at the huge maple tree and the leaves are so striking, so beautiful in color. It is a blustery Pacific Northwest Day. The leaves are falling and twisty-twirling to the ground. But now when I think of the sweet song, it does not bring gladness but a sorrow to my heart. Watching the ochre leaves fall, I should be happy, but the grief is deep. So deep....... Again.

Will this sorrow pass? When? My friends are worried. My husband is worried. Should I be? It is ok.... remember it is ok to feel the sorrow, to touch the sad and not be happy. It is ok.

# CHAPTER TEN

## YOU ALWAYS MISS WHAT YOU CANNOT HAVE…...

I found a birthday card that was meant to be sent to my sister with a gorgeous yellow birthday cake on the front, more quotes on grief and I found a sister's book- "SISTERS- Thoughts on that Special Relationship" that she gave to me in 1994-that was 21 years ago. I was thirty-eight. We had moved to the Pacific Northwest by then.

There were times we were not so close.

Especially when we lived nearby. I wanted to be. Her boys were older, mine just babies and I wanted to be close. She was weary, a full time working single mom supporting two sons that were showing the signs of NF. Mixed with the thought that I had the "perfect" children with no café latte spots (a possible pre-cursor to NF), larger than normal heads or bumps on their skin – I don't know.

I knocked on the door unexpectedly and she answered. She was not happy to see me. Eating her lunch and then leaving for work, she did not invite me in. I left and I felt so sad. I do not know why she did that. I will never know.

I share this to say that we were not always close. I was a baby and a toddler when she was 13 and 15. Always remembering the story when I got onto her bed, dumping powder and perfume on the bedspread. She was irritated and annoyed at me for most of my young life and I cannot say that I blame her.

Our relationship really changed when we moved away to the Pacific Northwest. You always miss what you cannot have. We began to understand; especially my sister, what we were missing. As the years passed, we became closer. We talked by phone often and we sent letters to one another....my children in the throes of adolescence and her boys,' young adults. Our hearts torn as we watched them struggle in their own worlds.

We tried to set up email and skype, but she had a challenging time with technology. She used her computer to play the game of solitaire. We lost our parents. We grieved together and made it a point even before they left to say that we will not fight over money, over the estate, nothing. We did not. We worked together. She bought my parents' house, the family home for over 40 years. Generational homes are common in Europe but not so much here.

So, it was just her and I for close to 16 years, talking about mom and dad, reminiscing about them. I no longer have that anymore. There is no one to talk to about my family.... maybe to my daughters... sometimes... but not really.

It really is a sad lonely feeling when your biological family is gone. Just gone....no more calls, no more letters or Christmas gifts.

Nothing.

It is then, we realize..... memory is the most precious of gifts.

Our memories fade or sometimes become unintentional in their perspective. Maybe we remember things better than they were or worse.... but memory can be a wonderful gift to our hearts and life. Remembering, though painful, is beautiful.

Another lone leaf falls. And another.... like memories in our lives......another and another.... Memories, bittersweet with sorrow. There is the bitter and the sweet.... the sweet will come, it is in the loving of one another....... the bitter, the loss.

"I cannot deny that, now I am without your company I feel not only that I am deprived of a very dear sister, but that I have lost half of myself." A quote from Beatrice d'Este's Victorian letter to her sister, Isabella d'Este.

And when you have lost half of yourself. Whether it be a lover, a sister, a child, a dear friend.... the grief is......it just is......

I saw my friend the other day. She knew my sister. She helped me with the living estate sale in Santa Rosa and then one after her death. She said she was going through some art supplies that I gave her, and she found two of Ginny's pencil drawings. I immediately understood the one. I had asked her to draw a cottage for me while I was living in Hope Cottage. We built that house to be charming and very cottagey. I would keep asking, year after year, about the cottage print and she would say, "I just can't do it. It's just not right." I told her she was being silly. I loved her artwork. And she said no, it's just not right.

I saw the cottage print when Leslie handed it to me. And, you know, she was right. When I first looked at it, it looked like a pueblo style home with wispy flowers in the garden. It was a yellow house with pinkish red flowers. It was not right but that made it even more perfect. I am going to get the print matted and framed as it will mean the world to me. Her artwork was never good enough for her.

I gaze at the view......the one she never saw.

The pink clouds hang low underneath the grey ones. Her artist's eye would have seen and translated the color to canvas. I speak in past tense.......

My eye can see it but not translate it to the canvas – only words that are never good enough. Oh well, such is life.

I ran into the store the other night-just a quick trip to pick up a couple of things. I had been doing well with my mood, my emotional grief. I walk in and what greets me on the end cap?? Full shelves of pink Almond Roca cans. My sister loved Almond Roca and I usually sent her a can every Christmas. Whoosh, the wind sucked out of me, the sadness descends, and I am there. I stare at the pink cans, and I am mad. I do not want to feel this way right now. But I am gone, engulfed into Griefland and my heart aches.

Another Christmas. Another Thanksgiving. Another year......

# CHAPTER ELEVEN

## HER OWN ART GALLERY

It is time to tell you about her art. I have most of it. I did give the neighbor a sea scape because they were so kind to her and watched out for her. I left them with the ocean picture and her tomato-soup red couch with all her eclectic pillows. They were so happy.........

For years, Ginny took private art lessons. She never called herself an artist, but she was. While visiting her years ago, I wrapped up her artwork in brown paper. Of course, now I have them and there are enough for all eight grandnieces and nephews. I will print the name of each one on the back and when they marry or get their first house, I will give these precious pictures to them. Each one picked for the personality of each child. I have one in my guest bathroom. It is a picture of an ibis with a dark navy-blue background; it is stunning. I love it!

My plan is to put all of them down the long hallway downstairs like an art gallery. She will have her own art gallery. I wanted to put pictures of her artwork in this book but that is hard to do and more costly. This is about words and her. Here are the subjects of her artwork. They are so tender and dear to me.

One year she created a still life depicting an imaginary shop that we owned, named V&C Hat Shop. It featured fancy hats in a window. I opened it at Christmas, thrilled and displayed it in my guest room, complimenting the vintage hats I collected.

Here are her other pictures that I have:

A still life of pears

Sonoma Vineyard

Russian-like peasant holding a chicken

Boat marooned upon the shore

A Road lined with Eucalyptus Trees

Several seascape's

Still life of vegetables

Closeup of an owl's face

The Fox

My Ibis

And a few more.......

You can tell she is an artist just by her subject matter.


November 28, 2015

After a nice Thanksgiving, we returned from Redding visiting our four adorable grandchildren. I was so busy cooking, cleaning, doing laundry, making gingerbread houses, peppermint bark and more, oh my.......... and prepping for the meal that I did not think of Ginny one time. That is what happens when you have a 10,7,4 and 2-year-old around. Now I feel badly about that, but this is part of the process. There will be times that the grief or the loss seems erased on the surface, but it is still deep in the soul and heart. I know that because of the depth of my feeling.

It is an icy morning. White frost covers the rooftops, the water looks cold. The harbor seals have come to visit early this morning. Sometimes, if I open the slider, I can hear their deep raspy barking.

The plan is to put up lights and decorate the house for Christmas over the next two days. I remember that Ginny never saw this house that she was so excited about…. excited for me. This would have been the 2nd Christmas of celebration if she had moved here……

# CHAPTER TWELVE

## A BEAUTIFUL STORY

I brought home all the items from her memorial service because I knew that I would be writing about that when I returned. I have the memorial book that her friends and neighbors wrote in. I have her large-squared calendar that I wrote the daily verses on as I journeyed in her loss. I have the cards and some of her diaries.

I am going to share the story of her loss now. And really, it is a beautiful story. It may be full of sadness, some anger, some wonder but it is also full of beauty and grace.

We had been talking about her moving to this area for years and years. She was so worried to lose her medical insurance because of her multi-faceted medical issues. I do not think this is uncommon for those with NF.

Finally-it was decided that she would move, yet we had to wait for about a year while she completed her health treatments. Tumors on her head had become cancerous and required radiation. I traveled to Santa Rosa so I could drive her to the treatments.

During this visit she had her 70th birthday, where we celebrated with a trip to Bodega Bay Lodge. We had room service, which she adored and never experienced. Also, we attended the wine hour and had such a wonderful time. She was so happy to be in such an amazing place.

Our dad, from his abalone days, placed the love of the ocean into our souls.

This was the perfect place to celebrate such a big event! We stayed in the rooms next to the ocean and it was beyond marvelous. She was so grateful and happy. I was so happy to see her so happy.

We loved Mendocino and Bodega Bay. I have not been to either place since her passing.

I will be taking some of her ashes to Bodega Bay next year. Some will be scattered here in Colvos Passage among the elephants swimming and some in Bodega Bay with the abalone shells clinging tightly to the sea rocks.

Fast forward from cancer recovery, a huge living estate sale, and a 70th birthday celebration. And now my husband and I are packing up the moving van to relocate Ginny to Washington State. I had found a wonderful place about a mile from my house for her to stay. It was so ideal. A one bedroom located in an adult community with a lovely dining room, classic pictures on the walls, art classes and outings to sign up for. A place to walk near the trees. Beautiful- just beautiful. We made all the arrangements, completed all the paperwork, and customized her living area. A beautiful place for a beautiful sister. Just one mile away from me.

Everything was ready.

We arrived in Sonoma County in Feb. of 2013 with only 4 days to pack her belongings and start on the journey to Washington state. She had barely started any packing. I do confess, I was a little irritated. With some of her friends helping us, we got to work. There was so much to do. I was also taking her to doctor appointments and driving her to visit friends to say goodbye. She was not feeling very well. Since her anxiety was heightened, I thought it might be due to that.

Two days before leaving, she stayed in bed all day. I took water and "sickie food" to her and thought she might have a flu bug. Then the next day, she felt better and was up and helping some with the packing. I felt so relieved. Then the night before our big departure, we were sleeping on a blow-up mattress in the guest room while she was on the couch in the living room because everything was packed.

I kept hearing her get up as she was using her cane for her balance. We were so exhausted from the packing up and cleaning of the house. Finally, after she had gotten up a couple of times, I managed to pull myself out of the low blow-up bed and go out to check on her. I knew, at once, something was terribly wrong. And without going into detail because it would embarrass her, I knew, without a doubt, she had to go to the hospital.

We had to call 911 and call for an ambulance. She did not want us to, but I kept telling her that she was not well and needed to be checked out. They put her on the ambulance gurney, and I bent down and told her, "I love you.... We will see you soon". She said with barely a whisper... "love you." I will never forget that whisper......

I wanted to go to the hospital right away, but my commonsense husband said they would be checking her in and running tests. We would not be able to be with her and we should go back to bed. I cannot even believe that I was able to sleep a few more hours. I was so exhausted from the packing. We then decided to go to the hospital. I did not go in, at first, because I have asthma. If I get a cold or flu, I have weeks of serious asthma complications so we decided that Dan would go in.

We were supposed to leave for Washington that day.


December 19, 2015

I interrupt this story for Christmas.

Oh Christmas! I love Christmas. I even have a book called "The Queen of Christmas" by Mary Englebright. I miss my sister so much at Christmas. I tried to make it special for her and we loved picking out small but meaningful gifts for one another.

I ran into Kohl's to try to find something to wear for Christmas but was unable to. I stopped in the middle of the aisle-gut punched- again but this time it was not the pink Almond Rocha cans.

This time it was a whole display of "Christmas Story" items. You know the hysterical "Christmas Story" movie.... Oh, how Ginny loved that movie and loved that leg lamp. She even bought one for herself. Of course, she did.

I stood. I looked and I felt deflated like a lost balloon whirling around the store. I was done. I was sad. I moved on but differently. The sadness hung like a little cloud above me. This will always be here, I thought. This is my life now. And I reminded myself that it was ok and that the process of grief is essential in building up a human being's character and heart. Especially the heart.

And I believe that with all my heart.

If I did not- I could not write about this path of grief.

Second Christmas without Ginny. Second year of grief layered upon my heart. Second year to remember the love. Our love. We deeply loved one another. That is a blessing beyond measure until we meet again in eternity. I will embrace this sorrow of grief and learn to walk this path.

I will choose to build my heart with love and lovely memories. I will choose the sorrow path that leads to more love. Because in so doing, I will get to love more and give more to the ones I love. And that will bring the joy.... the joy that is around the corner.... around the bend....... the next door.

December 28,2015

It is 3 days after Christmas. I really missed Ginny this year. We took Eila, our little 3-year-old granddaughter to her first Nutcracker Ballet. Ginny would have been with us. Caitlin, our little tomboy, is approaching 11 years old. She is dressed in a sparkly blue dress and Eila, in her silver tutu. All she could think of was twirling. Toward the end of the performance, she could not sit still. Standing up and twirling was beyond her control.

I could not blame her. Not because she could not sit still but because she only wanted to dance like a ballet dancer. My sister would have loved that. I loved that.

Another Christmas. Another sad season. You think I would have been thrilled this Christmas but the pain of almost losing my husband, after a heart attack and open-heart surgery, is too much. It is another reminder of missing my sister. Everything seems like it is more…. but I am looking for the joy that is around the corner, around the bend. I know it is there.

I went through Ginny's botanical themed recipe box and found some more recipes. This one fits the Christmas theme.

Remember I am typing them as they are written….

# Mary's Sees Fudge

4 ½ c. sugar

1 large can of evaporated Pet milk

Bring slowly to rolling boil 15-20min.

Boil 6 min. after it is fully boiling

Add one tsp vanilla

Pour this over 3 (12oz) pkg chocolate chips semi-sweet

1 large Pk miniature marshmallows

2 cups chopped nuts (probably walnuts)

½ cup butter stir until melted

Pour into buttered pan and cool

(Now we know you are supposed to cut them after they cool but there were no instructions for that…. but obvious, huh?)

So, another Christmas. # 2 without her. My heart hurts still….

This sounds good too!


Christmas Eggnog Cookies

2 ¼ flour

1 tsp Baking powder

½ tsp cinnamon

½ tsp nutmeg

¾ salted butter softened

½ c. eggnog

1 tsp vanilla

2 large egg yolks

1 ¼ c. sugar

1 tbsp nutmeg

Combine flour, baking powder, cinnamon & nutmeg. Mix and set aside. In large bowl cream sugar and butter. Add eggnog, vanilla & egg yolks- beat until smooth. Add flour mixture and beat until combined.

Drop on ungreased baking sheets

Sprinkle with nutmeg

Bake 23-25 min

3 doz

She does not say what temp for the oven, but my guess would be 350. These sound really yummy.........I think adding dried cranberries, grated orange zest and white chocolate chips would make these cookies divine. I might try them next year.

Next year will be year 3. I really do not like the sound of that.

My mind wanders back to that night, the night of the moving story.......

It's nearly midnight on a narrow street, crowded with parked cars, located near Santa Rosa Junior College. We had to move the 28- foot U- haul van at 3 in the morning. Back up lights and the beep, beep, beep sounds precede the arrival of the ambulance into the slender driveway.

She's gone.......to the hospital.

My husband makes me lay down and sleep for a few hours. He reasons that she will be checked in, admitted and a battery of tests run, and we will not get to see her. It is true but I want to be there. I fitfully sleep until morning. I wakened with a start.

We planned to leave today. It's Thursday. My husband needs to return to work on Monday. We decide to wait one day before finalizing departure plans.

# CHAPTER 13

## SHE WILL BE GOING HOME WITH ME

We go to the hospital and discover Ginny is being tested for the neuro virus and many other conditions. I am told I should go home and disinfect everything. We go back to the house and bleach-clean everything, wash all the linens and blankets, wiping down everything. We are completely exhausted. In our exhaustion, we are perplexed, worried and uncertain of the future.

We return to the hospital and wait.

I get to see her, and she is alert. I am hopeful she will recover. It will just take time. We can see that it will take time but who knows how much time. We make the decision that my husband will leave the next day for Washington state, and I will remain. I will stay in the empty house with the red tomato couch, blow-up bed, and one-fold up chair, pushed up against an outdoor patio table. It doesn't matter. I want to be here with her.

I have what I need. I will stay for however long it takes to move Ginny into recovery.

She will be going home with me.

It might be weeks, if not months, but she is coming home with me.

Today, while at my "killer view" home, sitting at my

desk, writing about these memories, I look out at the little turquoise tug, pushing its heavy load.

A sense of peace prevails as I watch it slowly work.

Reflecting on the past…...

My mind and heart go back to the hospital. I visit twice a day. My asthma has intensely flared up while sleeping on the cold wood floor of my teenage bedroom. My coughing will not stop. I am using my inhaler and realize that I am going under. I am by myself. I am the only one that can care for my sister. I am her power of attorney. Somehow, I must manage my asthma complications.

I have visited Ginny many times and Sunday is coming. Saturday was spent talking to the doctor and nurses about the documents listing her dying wishes. The nurse realized one section was crossed out, we did not understand why. We straightened it out and I was able to talk to both the doctor and nurse about my sister's desires for departing this world.

Or in their terms, the health directive.

For years, Ginny told me that she did not want to be resuscitated. She wanted to die naturally. She would even mention this randomly when we would be talking. And she would say something like, "And you know what I want Candy" and I would, of course, reassure her.

Jan. 7th, 2016

I resume my writing after last week's sessions and the unbelievable has happened. I wrote about the death bed scene at the hospital last week. I was so worn out; I ask my husband to take me out to dinner because I was thoroughly exhausted after I wrote about that.

Five pages are gone describing her death; disappearing into thin air. I remember being at page 72 and now it says 67.

I cannot even imagine writing that over. It was inspired. It was lovely, peaceful, and done. Done. I do not want to write it over again.

My husband texts me and says we will look for it tonight. Oh…. what a setback. I always see signs in everything. What does this mean? I do not want to write it over again.

I will wait….and ask my husband to help me find the missing pages. And if not……

I will rewrite it, be worn out again and be sad that those inspired words are gone……and, most likely, need to go out to dinner again. My sister would agree to that.


Jan. 12, 2016

I have not had the heart to write since I somehow lost

the most important part of my writing. Now I am even wondering if I woke up in the middle of the night and wrote it in my head and never typed it out. I was so certain that I had.

Anyway, back to the health directive.

And respecting Ginny's wishes.

Day 4 in the hospital and my husband is gone.

I have come back to the generational house that is empty. I decide to visit only once on Sunday due to my asthma complications. I told the nurse, when I left, if there was any change, at all, in Ginny's condition, I should be called immediately.


Feb. 21, 2016

I could not write for a while......again.

I was getting nervous that I might not be able to finish this story...... Take a deep, deep breath and begin.........

I received that call on Sunday night at about six. The nurse informed me that I needed to get to the hospital quickly, as soon as I could, safely. My legs were rubbery and shaking. I grabbed my purse and left, so thankful that the hospital was only 5 minutes away. Extremely upset and agitated, knowing that I needed to calm myself or I might have a heart attack or severe panic attack. So, I breathed deeply and told myself that

I would be of no help to Ginny if I was this upset. I felt a sense of scattered peace.

I arrived at the hospital, parked, and raced to the ICU as fast as I could. Ringing the ICU bell, a nurse accompanied me to her room. She stated we had to get there quickly. I could see my sister's room from a distance. There were way too many people in the room. That could mean only one thing. They had called a code on her.

Everything inside of me screamed… NO!!! I rushed into the room, and yes, there were about 8-10 people in the room……

Everything inside of me screamed… NO!!!

The charge nurse approached me and introduced herself, telling me what they were doing. I did not want to hear this… repeatedly, I kept saying to myself…. this is not supposed to be happening.

This is not supposed to be happening… over and over again. I was screaming on the inside and very, very emotional on the outside. I was shaking and there were hot tears.

A nurse was leaning over Ginny intubating her and I knew this was not good. This was not honoring my sister's wishes. I was still screaming on the inside…

The nurse explained to me what would happen if Ginny lived. She would have to go on dialysis and other stuff. I could not hear her words.

I told her that this was not my sister's wishes. I did not understand…. we had the health directive in place. This was when I could see "the look" on the faces in the room.

Real people just trying to do their jobs. I know they recognized my distress over my sister.  Looking at them, I said, "I know this is not your fault, you were only trying to do your jobs." I wanted to reassure them. I could not tell if they were upset because of my distress or upset thinking that the hospital might be sued. All I knew, is that I needed to reassure them that I understood their intensions.

Working out the details, the charge nurse told me that I would need to speak with the attending physician, by phone, who was caring for my sister the past few days. Previously, I had a conversation with the doctor, trying to be sure that everything was in place for the health directive.

On the phone, confused and dazed, something was missing – something I was not getting in my brain. I have not been exposed to much medical procedure so how would I know? As we were talking, she explained what needed to happen next. Nothing made sense….

I said, "well, can't we just take the tube out?" or something like that. She said very firmly, "no, that would be considered"…. (pausing)…. "Euthanasia."

Euthanasia by Wikipedia's definition is the practice of

intentionally ending a life in order to relieve pain and suffering. Euthanasia is legal in the Netherlands, Columbia, and Belgium.

I felt confused but she was the professional, so I had to accept this. She continued to explain what procedures would follow. Ginny would rouse herself and then they would remove the tube allowing her to pass. This would take about an hour or hour and a half.

I did not have a choice. Ginny did not have a choice.

I felt devastated on the inside. How could this happen? Why wasn't I here to stop this? The one day, I decide not to come to the hospital because of my pure exhaustion and asthma issues......Why? Why? Why?

So, enough of that, I told myself and went back into the hospital room and looked at Ginny. I felt so sad for her. This was not supposed to happen. I had a sense that I had let her down.

During the confusion and the chaos, I had to make the best of this situation. The sweet nurse who called me was in the hospital room, arranging items and explaining details to me. I think she could see I was in shock. I was stunned.

This was not the outcome I was expecting.

Bending over Ginny, I started talking to her. I held her hand and spoke some endearing words. Looking up at the nurse, she encouraged me saying that her father had passed the previous year in similar circumstances. She believed that patients in this condition, while not able to speak, can hear what is going on and understand.

In that moment, I decided, this was my time to tell Ginny how much I loved her. I told her very slowly and lovingly that I, Dan, Nichole, JJ, Chloe, Soren, Ansel, Laura, James, Jimmy, Caitlin, Brayden and Eila, all love her. We all love her. I repeated that to her at least 4 or 5 times during the time of her passing.

I told her stories, some of them silly. Like the time, when I was two, climbed on top of her bedspread and dumped powder and perfume on it. I think both my mom, and her, were very mad at my 2-year-old antics. Remember, she would have been fifteen at the time.

Memories of times we had spent together. Like the time we took a 3-day trip to Mendocino, our favorite coastal town. We were staying at an Inn and the lights went out. Pulling the heavy drapes back, we looked out the window. It was pitch black in the tiny town and we discussed the idea of a murder mystery. We both took turns telling the story and we scared ourselves silly. I think we both laid awake a long time that night trying to sleep with the thoughts of murder dancing in our heads. She loved mysteries.

I told her how wonderful heaven was going to be.....no more pain or sorrow or tears. I also told her that it was not fair that she got to go to Heaven before I did. I sang some simple songs to her......ones I could remember or recall and repeated some bible verses from memory. I really wish I had a recording of what I said because when I look back, I realize that it was incredibly sweet.

About halfway through the time, I stopped and laughed aloud and said, "I know, I know, you are thinking, Candy....would you just stop talking so much?".....and I laughed again.....

I kept holding her hand, stroking her greasy hair. The bumps on her head showing through the strands of silvery dark hair. And then, once again, I tell her that we all love her starting with me and going down the complete list. I said our names slowly with deep love. You were and are loved Ginny.

She began to rouse herself; her head began to turn but her eyes never opened. Sheer exhaustion was her companion now and she was deeply gone. I stayed... a moment more stroking her hair and hand. Turning, I left to get the nurse. I told her that she was waking up.

The nurse came in quietly. They removed the incubation tube. Less than 5 minutes, and my sister breathed her last breath on this earth.

She was gone......

This was her wish, this was her joy, and in my sorrow, I felt a deep joy for her.......

She was at peace now....... complete peace. No more ridicule or pointing fingers from small children in the store. No more adult eyes taking that second glance.

No more lights turned out on Halloween night......no more medical issues, cancer, melanoma, internal pain, balance issues, fatigue, depression, tumor removals, leukemia....no more.....done.

Done.

And she was going home with me.

# CHAPTER FOURTEEN

## THEN I REMEMBERED

I drove back to my sister's home, which had been my parent's house and walked in the door. Forty something years this small home had been in our family.

I called my husband and he cried with me.

I went to bed laying in the teenage bedroom of my youth and realized how I had been so upset about them intubating Ginny, bringing her back. I realized at that point; I would not have been with her at the end. The way it worked out enabled me to be with her at the end and to tell her all the stories, memories, and love. Especially the love.

My sister and I lived a long distance apart for 25 years. We saw each other once or twice a year at the most. We talked on the phone, wrote letters, sent gifts and flowers but mostly lived apart 340 days a year, every year for 25 years. So, to imagine that I would have the privilege of being with her during her last minutes on this earth was a blessing. This was a gift from God. I did not have that with my mother or my father. I was a long distance away from each of them when they passed.

I was with Ginny at the end. And I loved her so deeply. I was able to tell her that. How beautiful it was. I was no longer upset that the intubation had happened. I was deeply grateful that it had. Having this amazing last hour on the earth with my sister.......

I look out at the view of the water and there is a fat rainbow in the sky. A half- arch stretching across the muted grey clouds. It is softly fading......just as Ginny did that evening.......

March 4, 2016

I am no longer counting the days. It is the years now. Not the year but the years. Last night, in a panic, I ask my husband what the date was, he says, "the third" and I said, "oh today is the day....the day Ginny passed". He says "no, I think it was the 8th". I ask if he would go check and he did because he knew it was important to me. Coming up the stairs and into the kitchen, he is telling me that it was the second. "No!" I said, "not the second! I am sure it was the third". He quietly stood looking at me and I knew he was right; he had looked at the death certificate. The death certificate does not misplace the death of a person, a loved one, a beloved sister. But I had.

I do not know what that means except that I seem to be in a brain fog these days with plans of my husband's retirement around the corner and my eight grandchildren keep me remarkably busy. And life.... just life.

So, it happened, I missed Ginny's death anniversary. Maybe that was good for me. Maybe I should not dwell on it so much.......

Back to the story.

I went home to the empty house and cold childhood bedroom. I was exhausted with grief and tears but there was a strange peace in the house….in me.

The decision was made for me to stay on for the next two weeks and continue to take care of estate details and my sister's memorial celebration.

My days were taken up with plans for selling the house, visiting friends, cousins, and dinner with the next-door neighbors who had watched out for Ginny. I was planning for a unique but beautiful celebration of life service for my only sibling, my only sister, for the one I loved….love…..the past tense still does not work for my relationship with her.

There were friends and church people that helped with the celebration. I am sure they wondered why I was not having the memorial service at Ginny's church. Now, I even wonder but only a little bit. It was as natural as breathing to have the service at our family home. The generational home of 40 years. I was fourteen when we moved there. My parents lived there until they passed and now, my sister. This is where I wanted to be for the next two weeks. Saying goodbye and having some closure.

My parents are buried at the Franklin Park cemetery up the hill about 5 blocks from the house. I would walk up a couple of times and visit their gravesites. Another lost art of grieving in our culture. I would pick flowers from the yard and place them on the head stone. Ginny would not be there. Her desire was to be cremated.

The next two weeks, every day, I did something for the memorial service. I thought there might be only a handful of people there. It did not matter how many people would attend. What mattered was the love and care that accompanied the special details of this time for Ginny.

The house was empty. I had to gather tables from the neighborhood and the church allowed me to borrow their plastic chairs. All of Ginny's artwork was on the Kitsap Peninsula, brown paper wrapped, resting in my garage. The neighbor had one picture that we had given them for all the care they had demonstrated to Ginny. That was not enough artwork for the memorial.

I had my daughter, the artist daughter, the one so like Aunt Ginny, go in the garage and pick out three other paintings. The paintings arrived via FedEx, a few days later. My friend, Elaine, who is a master gardener brought flowers and vases. Another friend also brought flowers. Becky, one of Ginny's dearest friends sent a gorgeous bouquet of flowers for the fireplace mantel. The deep rich colors of burgundy and lime green contrasted beautifully…reminding me of the contrasts in my sister's life.

It was so important to me to have some memory of Ginny for guests to take home. There was nothing in the house and a token piece of paper or little cross from Michaels did not seem right.

Then I remembered…...

I remembered all the abalone shells that we had left in a large barrel in the back yard. My dad had hung those shells on the backyard fence. When I was younger, and way too influenced by what people thought, I was embarrassed by those shells hanging there. It was so ticky-tacky. I am glad our hearts and thoughts change because I now understand those abalone shells hanging on the old fence was the very essence of my father.

And they were/are the essence of my sister. I went out and opened the barrel and realized, yes, there would be enough.… I brought them to the outdoor sink under the patio and began the labor of love, cleaning them out. Shining them, scrubbing them, and gazing at the beauty of the shells was such a tender time.

I went to Michaels to purchase small candles, stick on jewels and beautiful cards, and wrote on each one Ginny's full name, date of birth, death, and a scripture verse.

In Loving Memory

Virginia P. McDonald

10 * 24 * 42 - 03 * 02 * 14

I wrote that on every card.… even now, it has a pain of beauty in the memory.

Remember the silliness of the butterflies? The last time Ginny had come to the Pacific Northwest for

Christmas, 15 months earlier, I had decorated my Christmas tree with a multitude of various colored butterflies. I wanted to surprise her. She walked into the room and there was my 12-foot Christmas tree covered with glittery butterflies and bulbs.

The tree was spectacular, and we laughed.

Oh, how we laughed. I told Dan where those butterflies were, and he brought them down when he came for the memorial. They would adorn the walls, tables, nooks, and crannies of the simple little house. They would silently watch and rejoice with me.

Butterflies, artwork, abalone shells, food ordered from her favorite local Italian deli and candy…. kids' candy. My sister loved kid's candy. So, I got all her favorites, licorice, Good and Plenty, spice drops, orange slices in honor of my mom, Smarties and more, much, much more. There was an entire candy table in Ginny's bedroom. I knew she would love that!!! She always used to say that she loved kid's candy and she did…….

This celebration of life service was perfect for my sister. Perfect in every way from the soft hymn music playing to the butterflies on the wall, her artwork, a beautiful book to write in, antique tablecloths that her friend Becky brought. I lined the walkway on both sides with the abalone shells, and each person selected a shell as they left.

Honor and love.

It was all about honor and love……

My husband and I did the eulogy.

It was more the memory of my sister than a eulogy. I shared the memories, while Dan shared the heavenly part with everyone.

# CHAPTER FIFTEEN

## VELVETTEEN RABBIT REAL

Over the next few weeks, I am going to write about the service, what was said and what was written in her memory book. To this day, I have not read the comments. I have waited. It was too soon to read them. I think I can manage after 2 years. Although it will touch places in me that I did not know existed. I already know that.

Grief can be fresh and old at the same time.

I am realizing now that I am about 80% done with this book, I am thinking about my next book. My sister tried to get me to write all these years and who would have ever known that it was her passing that would be the catalyst to get me going into serious writing. Not writing for a conference, poetry, (although poetry is extremely hard to write) or a newsletter but a real, REAL book. Velveteen rabbit real......

March 14, 2016

I put on the black sea socks with the swirling aqua and peach octopi on them. I hope they are my muse for the day. I know that Ginny touched them as she picked them out and that stirs the sadness mingled with the joy......enough to bring tears to my eyes.

I bring the bag that has the items from the memorial service and set it by my rustic desk. The desk which sits beneath the 6-foot-wide picture window that captures the most amazing view.

My eyes tear up again. Ginny was never able to see this house or the view.

# CHAPTER SIXTEEN

## "WRITING IS THE PAINTING OF THE VOICE....." VOLTIERE

The first thing I see is her address book, one I had bought for her as a Christmas gift. It is gold and has a floral Art Nouveau pattern on the cover. Inside are numerous addresses, friends, family, and practical services. All in a scrawled handwriting and not very well alphabetized. She was always embarrassed that she could not spell very well or alphabetize. I understand after researching about neurofibromatosis, her learning challenges were caused by this disorder.

Inside was a handwritten quote in her writing.


Ginny always loved the painting by Edvard Munch called the Scream. She saw herself in this painting. Finding this quote by Munch also brings to light some of her emotional landscape.


*"I was walking along a path with two friends the sun was setting*

*I felt a breath of melancholy*

*Suddenly the sky turned blood red*

*I stopped and leant against the railing deathly tired*

*Looking out across flaming clouds that that hung like blood and a sword over the deep blue -----and town. My friends walked on, and I stood there trembling with anxiety and I felt a great infinite scream pass through nature"* Edward Munch

Most of us are familiar with Edvard Munch's painting of The Scream 1893. Many people have a fear of this painting or find it too disturbing. Others, like my sister, found a strange comfort in this canvas of extreme anxiety. Munch, himself wrote on one of the copies of the painting....'Can only have been painted by a madman.'

"A majority of the works which Edvard Munch created, were referred to as the style known as symbolism. This is mainly because of the fact that the paintings he made focused on the internal view of the objects, as opposed to the exterior, what the eye could see. Symbolist painters believed that art should reflect an emotion or idea rather than represent the natural world in the objective, quasi-scientific manner embodied by Realism and Impressionism. In painting, Symbolism represents a synthesis of form and feeling, of reality and the artist's inner subjectivity.

Many of Munch's works depict life and death scenes, love and terror, and the feeling of loneliness was often a feeling which viewers would note that his work patterns focused on. These emotions were depicted by the contrasting lines, the darker colors, blocks of color, somber tones, and a concise and exaggerated form, which depicted the darker side of the art which he was designing. Munch is often and rightly compared with Van Gogh, who was one of the first artists to paint what the French artist called "the mysterious centers of the mind." **Edvard Munich and his Paintings. (n.d.) In**

**Edvard Munch-Paintings, Biography and Quotes. Retrieved March 14, 2016, from http://www.edvardmunch.org/index.jsp**

I believe that Munch's art and writing provided an emotional platform for Ginny's experience regarding her NF.

I never really liked The Scream. But now I am glad that Ginny had something that expressed her emotional landscape regarding her NF. Thank you, Edvard, for providing that for her.

Out my window, this day, this sky… is a heavy grey one. The clouds, a mix of dovetail grey and linen white are moving across the deep water of the passage. I really want to be a painter like Ginny was a painter. She could mix these colors and make them blend beautifully together on the canvas……. I can't do that.

But the other day as I was researching for my writing…...

I came upon the most amazing quote about writing that made me feel like a painter. Like my sister who was a gifted painter.

"Writing is the painting of the voice." Voltaire

I had an instant connection to my sister and her art when I read that quote. Oh Ginny, how I love you and miss you. I have your art......all of it except for the ocean picture given to the caring neighbors. I love your art. I hope, I pray that my writing is like your painting, your artwork......deeply beautiful......the painting of my voice...... For you.

March 28, 2016

There are seven windows in our third story bedroom. Mostly what used to be referred to as picture windows. This is an 80's house.  We finally had the money to put blinds on the windows. They had to be room darkening for the morning. Because I am my father's farm daughter, I wake up with the brilliant morning light shining through the windows. But I miss waking up to the view of the water in the morning. I need to remember how beautiful it is here and remind myself to open the shades for the morning view of the watery sound.

Grief needs to remember.

We need to open our hearts to the beauty of grief. It is hard. It is sad. It is the deepest loss, but the light comes. The light comes when we open our hearts to the light. Loss can stay dark and sad for ages, for years, for decades but when we open our heart... the smallest crack......the light shines through.

There has been more light seeping into the cracks of my heart. Have I opened my heart to the light or has time eased some of the sorrow? I really don't know.

I just know that I welcome the lightness of my grief.

What will I pull out of the memorial bag today?

I created a small, framed picture for the table where everyone signed the remembrance book. There are butterflies scattered around the page, glittered butterflies along with this poem.


Virginia Pearl McDonald

10-24-42**********03-02-14


Lover of Beauty

Kind, Generous

Artistic


Lover of Books

Brave, Creative

Peace-loving


But Mostly

A gentle Lover of God

I know, it might be strange. But now I can place this tribute poem on Ginny's shelf. Yes, Ginny has a small bookshelf hidden from all who enter my house. Unless they come upstairs to my bedroom. Outside the door is a small landing with just the right amount of space for the small bookcase that is really a memory case.

Other cultures do this, but I am not so sure we practice this in the United States. I remember that I want to bring honor and recall the love of my sister.........

On this little wooden primitive piece of furniture are pictures of Ginny, a family pic, a strand of glittered butterflies she gave me for my birthday, her incense burner, a necklace that my daughter made in honor of my sister's passing. The necklace has a tiny little bottle with lemon peels from my family's generational home. Just typing this brings tears to my eyes. There is a beautiful Willow Tree figurine that one of my dearest friends gave me at her passing. A woman's figure with her outstretched arms cupping a butterfly. The name of the figurine is Angel of Freedom (Allowing dreams to soar) .... a few other things, a giraffe picture frame with Ginny feeding a giraffe. We did this together in Northern California and slept outside in safari style tents. I gave her a simple silver ginkgo leaf signed by an artist for her 70th Bodega Bay birthday. It was a symbol of beauty and simplicity from me.

Looking up the meaning of the Ginkgo leaf now stirs a mingled emotion within me. I had no idea that the leaf symbolized longevity. I was only to have the presence of my sister for a year and a half after this gift was presented to her. How could I know? How could I know there would be such a brief time left?

"In Japanese decorative art, the ginkgo's distinctive fan-shaped leaf has carried symbolism along with its singular beauty: the ginkgo has been a symbol of longevity (the tree can live for a thousand years) and of a more profound endurance (four ginkgoes survived the blast at Hiroshima and are still growing today)." **"Why the Ginkgo?" - Smithsonian Education www.smithsonian**


This small Ginkgo leaf holds her eighth grade graduation card that I found the other day......Virginia P. Rodgers....... her bible, a canvas by Kelly Rae Roberts, another last gift to me from Ginny. We picked it out together in a shop in Montgomery Village in Santa Rosa. It is a mixed media canvas print with a rosy-cheeked young girl with brown butterfly wings, roses in her hair, a bird on the bodice of her dress and it says, "I Choose Hope." I have draped across the side of the canvas a necklace of small, dried, pink rose buds that Ginny made me, possibly 30 years ago. This necklace looks like it was made yesterday....it has barely faded.... there are tiny sapphire- blue and white seed beads between the rosebuds. Such Beauty....... made and touched by her.

I do know that the trend now is to get rid of all these types of things. To free ourselves, to become simple and unencumbered. Minimalism. If I did not save some of these things, I would lose the story of us. I am already dealing with loss. I cannot lose the story of us, my sister and me.

And her ashes. Yes, her ashes are there…. still in the box from the mortuary. I looked at the urns and boxes they had on display. Not caring for any, I thought I will find something later. The ashes still sit upon the bottom shelf from the Eggen and Lance mortuary…. the same funeral home my parents used. I walk past her every morning and every night. Sometimes, many times a day.

Ginny always wanted her ashes scattered in the ocean. Bodega Bay and Colvos Passage…. states apart from each other will be her final resting places. I will keep a tiny, tiny bit in a tiny, tiny box. In a small, lacquered box with a butterfly on top – bought in Maui for my sister's ashes. Beautiful…...

Now the butterfly poem picture that I made is going on the shelf. Honor and love………deep love.

# CHAPTER SEVENTEEN

## SO MAYBE YOU ARE THE ONE

Look what I found!

My sister tried Facebook. I tried to teach her so she could view the growing years of her grand nieces and nephews. Remember what I told her in the hospital room? That we all loved her, Dan, me, Nichole, JJ and Chloe, Soren, Ansel, and Lulu…. Laura, James, Jimmy, Caitlin, Brayden and Eila. We all loved her so much.

Look what I found! She had kept asking me to send pictures of the house and the view. I finally got some developed – no small feat since none of us do that anymore. I even wrote on the back of each photo with names, events, and dates. I did not do this for my own photos, but I so wanted Ginny to have these. Here they are…. about fifty photos, photos of all the grand nieces and nephews. Photos of us moving into the "killer view" house and photos of Halloween, Christmas, Lulu's birth, Brayden's birthday, Chloe, and my date to Barnes and Noble, Ansel's sweetness in PJ's.

Some of the messages written on the back of the photos…….

2013

"Laura Tobin (31) Birthday-Brayden and Daddy made the cake"

"Eila Tobin-age 13 months-Halloween-2013 'giraffe with tutu"

"View as you drive down the street-Gig Harbor-Fisher House"

"View from private beach"- "steps to the private beach"

"Jelly fish on the Gig Harbor Beach"

"Beautiful Pink Sky"- "View from our Bedroom" (my writing desk)

"Moving Day"- "Working on the GH House"

"Annual Tobin Gingerbread House Building"

"Pile it on Gingerbread Making"

"Laura and James enjoying a cup of Joe at our Christmas celebration"

"Eila loves her new froggy from Aunt Ginny"

"Jimmy enjoying Aunt Ginny's Christmas gifts"

"Caitlin with Aunt Ginny's "hair pretty"- that's what James calls it"

"Aunt Ginny's pink Christmas tree welcoming Eloise (LuLu) to her new home." Dec. 21, 2013

"Ansel playing ball with grandma"

"Chloe with her pop bead necklace. She loved the pop beads, Aunt Ginny!" – "Grandpa reading a book to Chloe and Soren."

"I adore this baby" Grandma Fisher says."

"Lulu "laughing" and enjoying Aunt Ginny's birthday gift."

"The best present under the tree" Eloise Grace Matisse -----5 days old"

You might ask why would I want to share this with you? I share these photo messages to help us understand the love. The love it took to take the pictures, send them in for prints, write on the back of each photo a description that I thought Ginny would enjoy and then mail them to her. She had them for 2 months before she left this world. And she loved them. She told me that she looked at them repeatedly.

And now over two years later, I am looking at them and feeling such a sense of care and love that I was able to send these to Ginny. That I loved her enough to take the time, the effort, the love. I could have loved more but this is one time, I got it right.

So, I guess when I say she never saw the house with the "killer view," this is true. She never saw this house in person, but she looked at these pictures often. They were treasured and cherished. Can you sense the deep love? Can we love our family, our friends like this? Can you do this for someone you love? You will never know how much something like this demonstrates a deep love, which is needed in our lives.

Off my soapbox…this is not a soapbox story – just a story of love.

I carefully stack the photos together and wrap them with Ginny's rubber band. I will take them to show Laura and the kids when I go to visit in a couple of days. I will explain to them how much Aunt Ginny loved them and these pictures. They will know her love through me.

I am coming to the end of this story, and it is feeling a tad sappy. I am at the hard part, the "things" in the memorial bag. Maybe this entire story is sappy………

I looked up sappy…. of course, I did.

"Sappy - adjective

"Used to describe something that is extremely emotional in an embarrassing way"
Cambridge Dictionary

I am coming to the end of Ginny's story, and I am emotional, but it is not in an embarrassing way. It is with grief, love, and honor. The reader understands. I understand.

To be honest with you…. I think it's the way it is meant to be… for me. It will be different for you…as it should be. But I am warning myself that I will not be sappy in an embarrassing way.

March 29-

It is gloriously sunny this morning, but it was so cold outside when we went on our walk. But the water is blue, the sunny- blue that makes the water sparkle. And the sky is a light blue with fluffy white clouds.

I am feeling what all writers feel when they are 80% done. I guess, what new writers feel. It is not any good. I can't share this with others. Why did I spend all this time writing this? At least, I have completed enough research to understand that this is a typical phenomenon during this writer's stage.

There are feelings of….

Should I quit? Should I work on something else?

No…. keep at it. This is not about me….it is about my sister and the love.

The deep love.

I have thought, all along, if one person reads this and is inspired to:

love more,

grieve well,

understand more,

stop and reflect on opinions about outward appearance…

It would be worth it, and I mean that.

So you could be the one.

I know, for sure, I have been the one to reflect and have so much more understanding.

## CHAPTER EIGHTEEN

CAN'T DECIDE WHAT TO NAME IT CHAPTER:
("Loved the Kill Bill Movies" or "Love One Another,
Deeply From the Heart")

Today I reach into the celebration bag and bring out a
folder with colorful butterflies on it. I used this at the
celebration service. Colors of teal, yellow, black, and
coral orange adorns the cover . I remember going to
Pacific Grove near Monterey, Ca with Ginny and we
looked at all the butterfly items. I wonder if that
butterfly store is still there. The monarch butterflies
come yearly to rest on the eucalyptus trees in Pacific
Grove Sanctuary.

I have always wanted to go there but I am never there
in the right month, October. Instead, we go to the small
town and walk the streets of Pacific Grove and dream
of thousands of butterflies. The folder was perfect for
her day.

The day of the celebration of life service, I looked out at
the people sitting in plastic chairs in the long living
room. It was not fancy, but it was warm and casual.
Her boys were there sitting toward the back, one
cousin and my husband. Everyone else were friends,
co-workers, and neighbors.

*"Thank you for being here. Each one of you touched Ginny's
life and she touched your lives. I am Ginny's younger sister,
Candra Fisher, known as Candy to most of you.*

*We are here today to honor and celebrate....*

*Also known as Cookie in our family, Ginger, Jen, and Jenny. To me she was always Ginny or Jen.*

*You have heard it said……. A sister is a forever friend.*

*That is mostly true. Because there is a 13-year span between us- I was four when Ginny left home at age 17.*

*I do not have memories of us at home but there is one memory that she and my mom would not let me forget. When I was 2 or 3, I dumped an entire container of powder and perfume in the middle of my sister's bed. I would think with that kind of reputation that my sister was ready to leave home. (a sweet laughter in the air when I shared that)*

*Ginny left home at age 17. She went to Santa Rosa Junior College and was certified as a Psych Tech. She worked at San Jose and Sonoma state hospitals. The job was challenging and a blessing at the same time. She had two boys, Lance, and Doug- that I still think of as boys, but they are grown men right now. (I paused and pointedly looked at Lance and Doug) Your Mom loved you both very dearly.*

*With a 13-year difference in age-the seasons of our lives were assuredly different. We especially became close when we moved to Washington State. Distance made our hearts grow fonder.*

*We talked by phone, wrote lots of letters and emailed for a while.*

*In order to remember Ginny, I will list her likes and dislikes……mostly her likes……*

*Ginny loved to read,*

*She was an artist-a talented artist (the pictures you see here were FedExed down here so there could be some of her work here).*

*She had an amazing style and was an eclectic collector--- only buying what she loved---her arrangements looked amazing.*

*She loved camels, butterflies (here I preceded to share the butterfly story of how we said if we began to like butterflies, we would know we were getting old because old ladies like butterflies. Well, we began to like them and neither one of us would confess our weakness for the lovely painted ladies until one day…. I spilled the beans and confessed. She laughed and said she liked them now. For years to come, we would buy each other little butterfly gifts, butterfly garlands, soap, candles, socks and more. And we would smile when we opened these little treasures).*

*Opals, her birthstone.*

*Flowers and vases-she had 127 vases at one time.*

*SpongeBob- or "Bob Bob" as my 18-month-old granddaughter calls him – more laughter….*

*Books with beautiful pictures……. Mystery books….*

*Kid Candy- there is a table of kid candy in her bedroom to honor her love of kid candy.*

*Amazingly generous- she would send money to help people that I would tell her about.*

*Loved Agatha Cristy.*

*She did not like vegetables or fruit except for asparagus and blackberry cobbler…. can you call that fruit? (Lots of laughter now)*

*I have a really cute story to tell you about her move up to be near us. We had found her a wonderful care home and it had a gorgeous dining room and served three amazing meals a day. The chef from the Peninsula Retirement community called the day before we were leaving and talked to Ginny. She asked Ginny what kind of food she liked and chatted with her for a few minutes. She was beaming when she hung up the phone. I looked at her and said…." La-di-da! Aren't you special?? I have never had a personal chef call me!! Aren't you all that now??" She laughed so hard and was so happy.*

*She loved sandwiches (so we have sandwiches today from her favorite Italian deli down the street; Canevari's).*

*She loved all things Australia. I helped plan a dream trip to Australia, for her, many years ago. I was supposed to go but with two small children and renovating a 100- year- old home, I did not have the money to go. I convinced her to go on the trip. She rode a camel, went to Ayer's Rock, and saw lots of opals, deciding to buy some of her birth stone. It was one of her most cherished memories.*

*Really liked the Kill Bill Movies- (this is when most people gasped but it was absolutely true).*

*Loved Skip-Bo-the card game.*

*Loved cookbooks…even sandwich cookbooks but did not really cook much.*

*Loved Gabe-her beloved cat of 12 years (and now I just want to take the time to thank Becky, one of Ginny's dearest friends for offering to take Gabe. I am so thankful and know Ginny would be so happy).*

*Loved Bodega Bay- for her 70th birthday, I treated her to the Bodega Bay Lodge, and we had room service and she loved it and the food. Many of you know that Ginny was a fussy eater. It must have been all those cookbooks she read. (More gentle smiles and laughter).*

*Loved French Braiding the girls, my two girl's, Nichole and Laura's hair for piano and violin concerts.*

*Loved feathers and collected them.*

*Loved cream puffs.*

*She loved trees, leaves and the fall colors. And leopard- yes leopard prints!*

*Loved God, God's Word and watching Charles Stanley.*

*She loved unique jewelry – cameos and especially abalone. (Please take an abalone shell as you leave…one per family…. this is to remember my sister, my dad, and his shells).*

*She loved Mendocino-that was our town. (I told the story of staying at the B and B and the lights going out in the entire town and how we made up a mystery story taking turns telling it….) I think we got a little scared that night.*

*She loved me and I loved her.*

*The nurses commented that it was so obvious that we deeply loved each other.*

*And we did.*

*We were blessed with a loving relationship.*

*It was a precious gift.*

*1 Peter 1:22 says "love one another deeply, from the heart"*

*And We Did.........*

*So, it is true.... A" Sister is a Forever Friend"- here on this earth and even when separated. She, in eternity and me still on this earth.*

*We are forever...*

*Our deep love will never fade, and sweet memories will shine in my heart forever".*

Eulogy by Candra Fisher,

My husband then went on to share about the Love of God and how Ginny would want everyone to know His love and to be with her in heaven one day. It was simple, sweet, to the point and so....so true.

After that I encouraged everyone to eat the delicious Italian food, partake of the kid candy table, sign the memorial book and then it was just a celebration of sharing stories and love. It was simple and so sweet....

just like Ginny would have wanted.

The flowers were beautiful from friend's yards, vintage tablecloths for the borrowed tables and her dear friend Becky sent a gorgeous spray of flowers for the fireplace mantel……..her favorite colors of burgundy, apple green and gold. Her pictures hung where people could see them and there was a picture of Ginny on her retirement day holding a huge bouquet of balloons, beaming that she was finally done with her challenging job.

As everyone left to go home, the iridescent abalone shells lined the simple pathway. A memory of such a beautiful person, such a kind sister.

Earlier, I shared some information about the abalone shell. It was not but a couple of months ago, as I was looking at one of the shells that my dad harvested, I realized something weird and profound. I have these shells scattered throughout the house, in the sunroom, in the dining room, by flowerpots at the front door. As I was looking at the shell, I realized how similar the shell and Ginny were. You see, the shell's outer form is rough, a ruddy pink and has numerous nodules on it or pronounced bumps. But the inside of the shell is so beautiful with whirls of colors, sea blue, green, purple, soft pinks, and silver in the most gorgeous patterns.

This was my sister. She had 100s of bumps on her outside body. To the untrained person, unable to perceive the beauty found in the seemingly ugly exterior. But looking on the inside of that same shell, of that unattractive person to the world..... my sister.....she was so incredibly beautiful and kind.... perfect in her form. If I could think of the most perfect word for beautiful.... I would use that word to describe my sister.

Here are some of the synonyms for beautiful:

Elegant, gorgeous, ideal, lovely, stunning, radiant, fair, fetching, exquisite, delicate, divine, fascinating, enthralling, magnificent, captivating, alluring

Maybe I could choose exquisite, fascinating, or lovely to best describe her.........

I will stay with the simple word, beautiful......because that is how I always think of my sister.......

I look up and one of the tugboats is pulling a huge barge load. There are tears in my eyes. Life is hard and we keep pulling our loads back and forth, back, and forth. My dear Ginny has no loads to bear right now. She is beautifully at peace. And that comforts my heart.

I want to write about these tugboats, more so about the people that drive them back and forth......carrying their heavy loads. Are their lives full of heavy loads? Does this work put it all in perspective? Do they love their job? Do they hate their job? Can they see what I see when I watch the barge travel?

Do they know that they inspire me?

April 25, 2016

Almost a month since I have written. There have been personal issues and life's craziness. In fact, I may have not written today but I found this word when I was doing some research for our retirement trip.

A hoodoo is a pinnacle, spire or odd-shaped rock left standing by the dynamics of erosion.

There are spectacular hoodoos in Bryce Canyon, UT which I will see for the first time in October. Again, my sister's birth month.

I am feeling like a hoodoo right now after the forces of grief and a near death episode of my husband. And then there is the rest of life.........without explanation.... It is unnecessary to explain.

It has been a month since I have written. That is a long time. I want to be finished. I am having the sense that it is time to be done. My husband will be retiring early because of a major heart attack and surgery. My adult children are pulling away from me for various reasons- mainly because their own lives are so full of four children in each of their families. And there are other reasons....many other reasons......unspoken reasons.

We are leaving on our retirement trip, and I have thought I might write about our adventure. Unexpected conditions causing us to make decisions early, causing us to reflect and pause on what is important to us. A way of inspiring someone else to do something early before the perceived time.

It is like these words, these words are to inspire us to love, to really love…..to care, create changes and be kind. And to realize that there is a certain beauty in the ugliest of things……in fact, there is a deeper beauty in the pain, in the ugly, in the not so normal.

We just need to look for it and honor it.

There are full days, even several days will go by and I do not think or grieve over Ginny. That seems, somehow, wrong. But I know it is so right.

It is the joy that I knew would be coming.

The crack of light in my heart.

# CHAPTER NINETEEN

## A BLUEBIRD SYMBOLIZES HAPPINESS

The house is full of Ginny's collectables. Each room holds various reflections of her. Laura, my daughter, sent a picture of rooster covers that she bought for her electric stove. She had to have these in memory of her aunt. Who does that except for a kindred soul of Aunt Ginny's? One of her works of art is a peasant woman holding a chicken. It is a simple expression of poverty and richness together.

On my desk, I unwrap more of her mementos. A small black box is covered in burgundy and rust folk-art images ....... leaves, little red berries, a montage of fruit....... and it has little treasures inside. Ginny's treasures.... a brass "Hear no evil, See no evil, Speak no evil, Monkeys" figurine.... a French Limoges box, miniature plate broach wrapped in white tissue. Tissue she touched.... now the tears come. They are still there. A moon pendant bought in Mendocino, our town, a copper beaded leaf.....an art deco silver broach with large gaudy rhinestones on it. Vintage....

I cannot part with these items.... I had them set aside to take to an antique store. No, I can't part with them.... Yet.

Last week, I found some little notes written by Ginny to me.... not one of them had dates.... bad handwriting and she could not spell but remember there were reasons for this. The Neurofibromatosis.

One is a UNICEF card with an exotic Parisian blue door on the front of the card. It must have arrived sometime after her 70th birthday because she was thanking me for her birthday weekend in Bodega Bay…. "With love and many thanks for the beautiful birthday you gave me…especially the time of yourself. Thank Dan too…he had to give you up for love and care to Nichole and sister-in-law." Isn't that sweet? I told you that she was kind.

As I read these little notes, I see a pattern of her saying lots of love and thanks in each one. That was a new expression for her. She was sending me love because she knew she would not be on this earth very much longer. Oh Lord….my heart misses her.

I found a card I sent to her on Feb. 6th, 2014-less than a month before her passing.

It is a Trader Joe card with a block print of bluebirds and in the inside, I wrote this…

On the left-hand side, I wrote "A bluebird symbolizes happiness. It is a widely accepted symbol of cheerfulness, happiness, prosperity, hearth and home, good health, new birth, the renewal of springtime." Internet ASK

*"Dear Ginny-Hi! I am sending you some blue birds of happiness! It is my prayer and hope that you are very happy in Gig Harbor, and we will only be a mile from each other.*

*(a smiley face) We will be seeing you soon. With lots of Love,*
*Candy*

I sent her many cards and called over the course of the month before her planned move to Washington. She expressed how much it meant to her.

So today, I pull out of the bag, the memorial book I bought for people to write in.

It has a beautiful sage green silk-like cover with ferns and wildflowers embossed in silver. It says A LIFE remembered.

In Loving Memory of

Virginia P. McDonald

10-24-42  -  03 - 02 -14

There are some sympathy cards in the book and people wrote memories about Ginny. There are cards not even opened.

I can open the cards now. One homemade card said… "Ginger left a legacy of kindness." Others felt this and saw this……how lovely that is…...

One of the cards has wheat blowing in the wind and says "Let, I pray Thee, Thy merciful kindness be for my comfort." Psalm 119:76

Inside this card, a dear friend of Ginny's wrote this…. "I will truly miss Virginia and the good talks we had, and we both enjoyed eating out. The Lord shortened her sufferings from all of her health problems. I'm just sorry that she didn't get to spend at least some time closer to you and your family. I look forward to seeing her again in the next life where there will be no pain and suffering and we'll have new bodies that will see no diseases. Today we celebrate God as he made the special person that Virginia was!"

I just finished reading all the comments and I will list just a couple. I did not write in the book at that time. I could not. I can now and I will.

"The most caring and thoughtful mother a son could have. I will miss your love and sense of humor. Love, L.M."

"Ginny, (Cookie)... (yes did I share that Ginny had the nick name Cookie as a child and mine was Candy?) To your cousin- you were so sweet and loving. I remember when I was a young girl- you... holding me in your arms. You will be missed dearly.... All my love, G.J. -2014"

"I met Virginia about 20 years ago at Bethel Baptist Church, now Crosspoint Community. She always had a kind word and a smile for everyone." C.B.

3-15-14 "I met Virginia one day in Macys close to 30 years ago. That doesn't seem possible. We became good friends right away sharing the same disorder, NF. We were able to talk about all our fears for our children having passed the disorder on to them and our – fears and trials living with NF. She was lovely, kind, sweet, sweet lady whom I loved knowing. I will miss her but find comfort in knowing she has found true peace." N.B.

"To A Mother that was very caring and giving She was an inspiration to a lot of people and would help a lot of friends, and also she would help some people she did not even know… I have to say I am very Happy to have a very loving and caring mother and know she has a lots of friends family that care and love her so much -I will miss her so much" - D.M.

Interesting that D.M. wrote like his mother, run on sentences, no periods, lots of capital letters where they do not belong, but he wrote from his heart…his love for his mother.

I pulled out an 11 by 13 framed picture of Ginny on her retirement day. Her dear friend Becky printed it out and brought it to me for the Celebration of Life service. She is so happy on this day holding a bouquet of balloons and waving. You can see the nodules on her hand and face. Such bravery…. you know…. such bravery……such happiness on her ------ face.

There was so much struggle in her life but in the struggle, she found ways to be kind and caring. She could have been bitter and resentful. Honestly, she had every right to be. Yet, God captured her heart, and she chose to be brave, loving and kind by God's grace. If she can…..can't we??

There are three little journals that I found while going through her items. One was a journal from when she went to Australia. It was her lifelong dream to go. I was supposed to go with her but could not financially afford it, so I helped her plan the trip and she had a marvelous time. She saw Ayers Rock rode a camel and went over the bridge in Sydney. I am always so happy that she went. She so loved the movie., A Town called Alice. Her dream was to see Ayers Rock and she did. I am so happy that I helped her to accomplish her lifelong dream.

I read her journals, and they reinforced my knowledge of her depression and her lack of feeling like a worthy person. This makes her more brave and more worthy than most people I know. More worthy than myself.

I slept the sleep of grief after reading her journals. There were not many pages, three small journals, all incomplete, many years in between entries, forty pages at most. Her sorrow reflected; her pain of life expressed....... her trying to work it out. But how?

It is a mystery of God....... she had NF, I did not. I could have had NF; she could have not. A mystery...

Many of her thoughts regarding unworthiness and the deep depression that she experienced were in her early years. Her anxiety further deepened as she grew older. She had so many fears and deep insecurities, yet at the same time, I see these challenges added a depth to her kindness and to her as a person. This made her who she was. In our young years, we cannot see that the challenges and struggles will add a certain depth and beauty to our lives. I honor my sister by keeping most of this writing of her secret heart a continued secret. She would not have liked her words shared for people to read.

Ginny had that depth and beauty, while experiencing deep pain and sorrow.

Beauty.

Just Beautiful.

# CHAPTER TWENTY

## I SAW HER HEART

As I look back on our relationship, I realize that I was the cheerleader. I was the catalyst that helped spark some of her dreams and desires, a trip to Australia, art lessons, travel to the PNW, and buying a house. She needed a cheerleader, a sister who loved her with all her heart and always wanted the best for her. I needed her love and care. Her patience with her younger bratty sister. Her constant, caring love. Her kindness.

I was a sister that often had a critical yet loving heart toward the realities of her life, someone living with a constant medical condition. I could not comprehend how this would sink into the heart, into the life of a person.

Could this be because I did not see the NF in my sister?

I did see her heart, her love, her pain.

But the "bumps" as she called them, the NF, I did not see.

The creamy- white tug is slowly pushing a large barge holding concrete pillars. It is such a large load for such a little tug. Yet, the tug is swift and full of purpose. The barge and tug flow along with the current. A load will be unloaded, and the tug will return for another cargo. The cycle repeats itself... Again and again.

We learn that there will be heavy loads in life, all will

need to press....back and forth....back and forth. Then we realize that there are some that quietly push their loads, undertaking this with a fierce commitment to kindness and love. They do not murmur in their pain; they do not regret......

The love of God is settled on them.

I will share one page from Ginny's journal. This is what she learned through all the pain, the suffering, the ugliness for which she was ridiculed.

She would want us to read this page and take it to heart. Oh, the beauty of it......

This entry was wedged between a May 1993 entry and an Oct. 1996 entry. It is undated.

*"That if my children ever read this, know you my children...I love you both very much....my mistakes.... I am sorry for.... cannot change them.*

*Remember you are the only one that can change your life. Only change for the better if you can. (You can)*

*Cannot pull this through each day...often only once in a great long time, do I feel ... within me.... what is true...we are our own enemies if we allow it.*

*Love yourself L and D in the manner that you accept yourself.*

*What is important is what is inside.*

*I CANNOT LIVE THAT EVERY DAY BUT I KNOW THAT IT IS TRUE."*

Her journal continued:

May 2, 1993

*"Went today to a celebration of life party. Ron a nice man at work who has just went through chemo and bone marrow transplant.*

*I could cry here...I am feeling to my very depths such unresolved feelings of self – pity (ugly feelings) when this man and his family show such courage and love for each other. Very uplifting."*

No, Ginny you were very uplifting. (& will continue to be for those who read your story)

You had the courage to be brave amid the midst of deep pain.

And you loved me so very much....... I have had no other love like a sister's love......

You rose above your personal circumstances and helped others, not in huge ways, but in ways where simply knowing you......people in need, friends, and family, felt the difference, felt the kindness and the love.

And you were so kind....so kind....

I am so thankful for the gift of your life to my life.

We did deeply love one another......We do deeply love one another…...

I love you my dear sister and I always will……...

My last quote for you, for me, for all of us together…….a whispered prayer……

"I know now that we never get over great losses; we absorb them, and they carve us into different, often kinder creatures." – Gail Caldwell

## AFTERWARD

February 15, 2019

"Kindness

Noun: kindness

The quality of being friendly, generous, and considerate

Synonyms: kindliness, kind-heartedness, warm-heartedness, tender-heartedness, goodwill, affectionateness, affection, warmth, gentleness, tenderness, concern, care." Dictionary-Definitions from Oxford Languages

In just a few days, it will be 6 years since my sister has passed from this world. Currently five years that sometimes feels like yesterday and sometimes feels like 50 years ago. My phone calculator tells me that 6x365 = 2,190.

2,190 days of missing and still deeply loving my sister. The elusive joy has come when I see Almond Roca cans or abalone jewelry.

Now, a small smile comes to my mouth and heart.

And I always remember that we really loved each other.

The greatest joy is the ever-present memory of really loving one another.

Ginny………..

Thank you for the love.

Thank you for the kindness.

"Constant kindness can accomplish much. As the sun makes ice melt, kindness causes misunderstanding, mistrust, and hostility to evaporate."   - Albert Schweitzer


Sept. 19, 2019

I do not count the days now.

I count the years

I am traveling to Bodega Bay to take my sister's ashes to a place she loved. A place she called home away from home.

My husband and I are in our travel trailer for two months on this journey. A journey of love to honor my sister.

It is fall time. Our favorite time of the year.

The grief journey has softened into moments of extreme joy. The joy of a trip to Portugal, joy of my grandchildren bringing such happiness, delight, and laughter into my life.

My husband now talks to me about our mutual grief. Not allowing me to wallow in the thinking, he reassures me that I have not waited too long to scatter her ashes. Nor too long to finish this book.

He just simply said, "Now is the time...." The one who laughed at my "shards of glass" comment understands more about grief now. He was grieving too. In his own way and path.

So, we are here. We will be in Bodega Bay in a few days, and it will be time.....


Jan. 28,2020

6 years, soon to be seven.

I do not usually dress for writing but today I put on the sea socks that Ginny bought for my birthday. These socks have orange sea stars like the ones at Cannon Beach and tan silver dollars. I did not kiss them today, but they make me smile. I wear the abalone earrings that I bought in a Bodega Bay shop. The shop owner's mother, a local artist, created them. The earrings are stunning; one of the few abalone pieces where the pink is pronounced in the small of the shell. Stunningly beautiful and unique.

I found my journal from our 2019 fall West Coast trailer trip, and I am ready to write about leaving Ginny in Bodega Bay. It is time.

Did you know that there is a copious number of ashes created from the body of a deceased person? About five pounds for an adult. I did not know that. I was surprised. I also did not know that I would not easily be able to scoop her ashes into a bag that we would take down to the water. Some of the ashes got on my thumb, while it did not freak me out, it did make me feel incredibly sad.

I cried. Really sobbed.

Some notes from my west coast trip. (unedited)

Sept. 27th-Oct. 1st, 2019

*"We arrived at Sonoma Coast State Park after a rough drive on Old Redwood Hwy. We drove past Cazadero and the Russian River area. The weather is nice, and we have a sandy spot to camp. We hear the foghorn every morning."*

*I always pick a word for the year to focus on. For 2019, it was Cherish.*

*"Now we are in Bodega Bay to scatter my sister's ashes.*

*I Cherish        Our Love*

*I Cherish that I have a husband who supports me on this memorial trip of Cherishing My Sister….."*

*I visit my childhood home and city of Sebastopol, California. I am shocked that I still love it. It feels like it has not changed that much in over 40 years. I find much joy wandering the streets and visiting little shops, going into my childhood library, and driving past my childhood home. The apple orchard is gone, a sub-division takes its place.*

More words from my journal…..

October 1. 2019

*The Day*

*Taking Ginny's ashes to Bodega Bay.*

*We drove up and down trying to decide which beach. I think Ginny would have liked the name Portuguese Beach, but it was not as pretty in comparison to the secluded cove on Schoolhouse Beach. There were rocks nestled in the cove and waves crashing against them. North Salmon Creek Beach was a long spectacular beach with too many surfers and people walking. It was crowded. Ginny was not a crowd person.*

*I have been reflecting on her 70th birthday. That would have been in the fall of 2012.*

*I took her to the Bodega Bay Inn for two nights. We had a bungalow by the sea next to the marsh lagoon. This was the first time she had room service and loved it.*

*Her gift was a small silver ginkgo leaf plate that was designed by an artist. We also went to the wine reception area and chatted among the "beautiful people" She never felt "beautiful," but she was amazingly beautiful on the inside.*

*We had such a wonderful time. We went down to Dillion Beach and sat on a bench and took in the view. She was not walking very well at that point.*

*Two chocolate brown Bodega Bay Lodge mugs rest in my trailer. She bought one and I bought one during her birthday celebration. I use them on our trips. A precious memory.*

*Back to the cove......a woman sitting on a driftwood log and her dog, a fisherman with a plaid shirt in the cove, fishing, reminded me of her son, Doug.*

*We peered down the steep slope of Schoolhouse Beach and saw the most beautiful, secluded beach with jagged black rocks and dramatic waves coming in. We walked down the steep path, me with my walking sticks, Ginny in her gift bag (We did not know what to put her in, so we put her ashes in a plastic bag and placed that inside a gift bag we had in the trailer) that said, "I wrapped this myself." Flowers on top-inside the bag.*

*I had it all planned to throw a flower, from each person, into the waves. Nichole, Laura, Mom, Dad, and us. Red rose from Dad (he grew them in his yard), pink carnation from Mom (she grew them at the Apple Orchard House) lime green chrysanthemum from Laura (her favorite color), and cream baby's breath from Nichole. (she is a cream girl)*

*We got up on the rock with a little seat as the tide was rushing in. We got concerned about a sneaker wave coming in. Suddenly the waves were crashing in. I told Dan to dump it fast and I was throwing the flowers in, not one by one, not saying this is from each person, but quickly. I threw them all in at one time.*

*We then, quickly jumped off the rock and backed away-took a selfie-laughing that we had turned our back on the ocean. Something that my dad, the avid abaloneer (my made-up word), always said never to do.*
*We went and sat on a driftwood log and looked out at the ocean, at the cove for a few minutes, gazing at the flowers as*

*they drifted away.*

*Back up the hill with my walking sticks (I had fractured my leg in four places after returning from Portugal, the surgeon placing a steel plate, eight screws and a band at the ankle). I took an amazing picture of the cove and after not finding an affordable picture in a gallery, we may have this picture gallery wrapped on a canvas.*

*We had thought about going to The Bodega Bay Inn for a shrimp cocktail and a drink. This is where I had taken Ginny for her 70th birthday. But the young man at the wonderful Sonoma Coast Visitor Center had shown us the deck that rested above Bodega Bay and said we could bring a picnic and a bottle of wine there. It had a nice chocolate brown, Ginny's favorite color, rattan couch, with mustard and pumpkin colors for fall and blue cushions.*

*We had gone to the recently renovated Tides restaurant. It was not the same. It had lost its appeal to us for wanting a celebratory meal. In the attached store, they had 4.99 shrimp cocktails that came in cute red and white checked bowls, with the yummiest cocktail sauce, shrimp, lemon wedge and oyster crackers. You mixed it yourself. Dan got extra sour dough bread. We took the shrimp cocktails and Trader Joe wine to the deck and enjoyed our picnic and watched the pelicans and harbor seals in the bay.*

*We toasted "To Ginny" with a smile on our lips.*

*We stopped at some art galleries, one that Ginny and I had been to.*

*I bought some abalone earrings made by a local artist.*

*Beautiful pinks…*

*We headed back to the camp and made French onion soup in honor of Ginny. Well, I microwaved Trader Joe's French Onion Soup and we had a toasty blazing fire our last night in Bodega Bay.*

I watched the stars come out

One by one

And thought of Ginny

In her

Beautiful

Secluded

COVE

And my heart

Smiled………..

We really loved each other

The kindness legacy continues. I watched my 7-year-old, granddaughter, Eila extend the sweetest gesture to her best friend, Gracie and I thought…

let the kindness flow…

Thank you, Ginny, for your living legacy of kindness…

Thank you…

The kindness lives on.

ACKNOWLEDGEMENTS

Gratitude.

I have so much gratitude to so many regarding this story of a beloved sister.

My mother listened to my stories outside while we ate triangle cut sandwiches and drank sweet tea. She always took the time to listen.

My dad was kind and contributed a legacy of kindness to our family.

Of course, this whole book acknowledges a sister and our love. Thank you Ginny.

A husband for 45 years knows you inside and out. Thank you Dan for helping this "creative" writer with the editing.

To Susan and Steve Jones for reading, editing, and supporting me. Also thank you Paula Davis for being a reader and your encouragement.

Thank you Laura Fisher Tobin for taking the incredible abalone picture that graces the cover.

I am grateful to all my friends that encouraged and prayed for me along the grief path.

Lastly, all the honor is given to the Lord and his loving presence with me on this incredibly beautiful grief journey.

About the Author- Candra Fisher lives in and loves the Puget Sound region of Washington state. She writes on an old, whitewashed farm table on the 3rd story of her home overlooking the water where whales, seals, tugboats, cargo ships and sailboats move through the passage. She is a retired special education paraeducator. Loving to travel, read, write, support Fair Trade ministries and spend time with her 9 grandchildren is only part of her passion. Her poem, "Queen Anne's Lace" is published in "The Mom Quilt, stitching together stories of motherhood, hope & love."